Passing the PRINCE2 Examinations

The APM Group,

based on the original book

by Ken Bradley

London: TSO

information & publishing solutions

Published by TSO (The Stationery Office) and available from:

Online
www.tsoshop.co.uk

Mail, Telephone, Fax & E-mail
TSO
PO Box 29, Norwich, NR3 1GN
Telephone orders/General enquiries: 0870 600 5522
Fax orders: 0870 600 5533
E-mail: customer.services@tso.co.uk
Textphone 0870 240 3701

TSO Shops
16 Arthur Street, Belfast BT1 4GD
028 9023 8451 Fax 028 9023 5401
71 Lothian Road, Edinburgh EH3 9AZ
0870 606 5566 Fax 0870 606 5588

TSO@Blackwell and other Accredited Agents

The information contained in this publication is believed to be correct at the time of manufacture. Whilst care has been taken to ensure that the information is accurate, the publisher can accept no responsibility for any errors or omissions or for changes to the details given.

PRINCE® is a Registered Trade Mark of the Office of Government Commerce in the United Kingdom and other countries.

The PRINCE2 Cityscape logo™ is a Trade Mark of the Office of Government Commerce in the United Kingdom and other countries

PRINCE2™ is a Trade Mark of the Office of Government Commerce

The Swirl logo™ is a Trade Mark of the Office of Government Commerce

A CIP catalogue record for this book is available from the British Library
A Library of Congress CIP catalogue record has been applied for

First published 2007

ISBN 978 0 11 3310845

Printed in the United Kingdom by The Stationery Office, London
N5638481 C40 11/06 319042 19585

Contents

Foreword

This book is aimed at easing the path for all those intending to take the APM Group PRINCE2 Foundation and Practitioner Examinations. Those taking the APM Group Practitioner Re-Registration Examination will find that the advice provided is equally relevant and useful. *Passing the PRINCE2 Examinations* has been updated to reflect the changes to the PRINCE2 reference manual released on 31 May 2005 and the new-style objective testing Practitioner Examination.

Thanks go to the APM Group and the PRINCE2 Examination Board for allowing the use of PRINCE2 examination material, and Richard Pharro for his support and encouragement in getting this publication to print.

I hope that you will find this book of real use in preparing for, and passing, your examinations. The royalties from this book go to the APM Group annual PRINCE2 award scheme, full details of which can be obtained from the APM Group.

This is a complementary, not a 'core', publication on PRINCE2, and therefore is not endorsed by the PRINCE2 Examination Board.

Based on an original idea by Ken Bradley

September 2007

The PRINCE2 syllabus 2007

Introduction

This syllabus is designed to provide a basis for accreditation of project management professionals. The syllabus is based on the OGC publication *Managing Successful Projects with PRINCE2* (2002, 2005), and is intended to provide a basis for setting examinations at Foundation and Practitioner levels. Table 1 describes the competence required at each level.

Table 1 Competence required at each level of the Foundation and Practitioner Examinations

Foundation	This level aims to measure whether a candidate could act as an informed member of a project management team on a project using the PRINCE2 method, within an environment supporting PRINCE2. To this end they need to show they understand the principles and terminology of the method. Specifically, a candidate should be able to:
	• describe the purpose and major content of all roles, the eight components, the eight processes and the techniques
	• state which management products are input to, output from, and updated in the eight processes and the sub-processes of Controlling a Stage (CS) and Managing Product Delivery (MP)
	• state the main purpose, and key contents, of the major management products as identified in the detailed syllabus
	• state the relationships between processes, deliverables, roles and the management dimensions of a project.
Practitioner	This level aims to measure whether a candidate could apply PRINCE2 to the running and managing of a project within an environment supporting PRINCE2. To this end they need to exhibit the competence required for the Foundation qualification, and show that they can apply and tune PRINCE2 to address the needs and problems of a specific project scenario. Specifically, a candidate should be able to:
	• know or comment on detailed explanations of all processes, components and techniques, and worked examples of all PRINCE2 products as they might be applied to address the particular circumstances of a given project scenario
	• demonstrate that they understand the relationships between processes, components, techniques and PRINCE2 products, and can apply this understanding
	• demonstrate that they understand the reasons behind the processes, components and techniques of PRINCE2, and that they understand the principles underpinning these elements
	• demonstrate their ability to tune PRINCE2 to different project circumstances.

Note: The ticks in the right-hand columns in the syllabus show what topics are included in the two examinations. The numbers in the 'Level' column refer to the levels as defined by Bloom's Taxonomy of Learning, which provides a useful structure in which to categorise test questions. There are six levels in Bloom's Taxonomy, but level 5 (synthesis) is currently not tested within PRINCE2.

This syllabus is correct at the time of going to press.

The syllabus will also inform the design, development and use of training materials and courses aimed at raising an individual's understanding of and competence in the project management approach as described in *Managing Successful Projects with PRINCE2*. The syllabus has been designed with ease of reference, extensibility and ease of maintenance in mind. The structure of the syllabus is depicted in Figure 1.

Figure 1 Syllabus structure

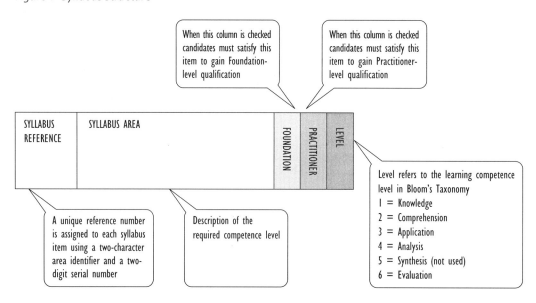

Explanation of levels (Bloom's Taxonomy)

The Practitioner Objective Test Examination is designed to use computer-aided assessment to test the PRINCE2 Practitioner syllabus. This format uses objective test questions which require a student to choose a response to a question from a set of choices for which the correct answer is pre-determined.

The Practitioner Examination demands a greater level of understanding and application of the method than the Foundation which largely tests knowledge of principles and terminology of the method. A column has been added to the syllabus section tables below to indicate the different learning competencies tested by the Practitioner Examination. This is a classification based on Bloom's Taxonomy, which is widely used in education and the design of assessments (Bloom *et al.*, 1956, *Taxonomy of Educational Objectives*).

Each learning level requires a higher degree of competency to answer and can therefore be assigned a difficulty level to assist with question combination and the creation of papers of similar difficulty. The learning levels or competencies are:

1 Knowledge

2 Comprehension

3 Application

4 Analysis

5 Synthesis (not used)

6 Evaluation

Level 1: Knowledge

Knowledge is defined as the remembering of previously learned material. This may involve the recall of a wide range of material, from specific facts to complete theories, but all that is required is the bringing to mind of the appropriate information. Knowledge represents the lowest level of learning outcomes in the cognitive domain. Examples of learning objectives at this level are: knowing common terms, knowing specific facts, knowing basic concepts and knowing principles. In PRINCE2 terms this learning level maps to the syllabus statements 'know'. For example:

- know what part of a product lifespan is covered by PRINCE2 (OV05)

- know the purpose of Organisation (OR01)

- know the products involved in the controlled start of a project (CO3)

- know the products of Quality Management (QU03)

- know the products of Configuration Management (CM04)

- know the purpose of the Business Case (BN02).

Level 2: Comprehension

Comprehension is defined as the ability to grasp the meaning of material and interpret information in one's own words. These learning outcomes go one step beyond the simple remembering of material, and represent the next lowest level of understanding.

In Practitioner terms this is the demonstration of **understanding of PRINCE2 concepts** tested through interpretation of wording that is different from the standard paragraphs in the PRINCE2 manual or interpretation of a project scenario. This competency maps to syllabus statements 'understand'.

Candidates are not required to know by memory all the detail of that topic. For example, for the syllabus topic 'Candidates must understand the Configuration Librarian role CM06', we would not expect candidates to know by memory the list of CM responsibilities. However, their knowledge of the purpose of CM (CM01) and understanding of the overall purpose of the role would enable them to identify valid CM activities within a list of CM and non-CM activities.

Examples of syllabus topics that match this learning level are:

- understand the purpose and responsibilities of the Project Board, Project Manager, Project Assurance, Team Manager and Project Support (OR06)

- understand the content and purpose of a Project Issue, Request for Change, and Off-specification (CC04)

- understand the purpose, types and application of tolerance (CO07).

Level 3: Application

Application refers to the ability to use learned material in new and concrete situations. This may include the application of rules, methods, concepts, principles, laws and theories. Learning outcomes in this area require a higher level of understanding than those under comprehension.

In Practitioner terms this maps to the **application of PRINCE2's components, techniques and products** to a given project situation and the syllabus statements 'apply a component or technique', 'create', 'modify' or 'demonstrate the application'.

In the objective test format candidates can, for example, be tested on the creation of products using 'matching questions' which require the candidate to match statements to the correct product composition heading.

Other possibilities include testing PBS/PFD creation by using partially blank diagrams for which candidates have to identify correct products from a list to match the blank product.

Examples of syllabus topics that match this learning level are:

- design an appropriate organisation, applying all roles as identified in PRINCE2 (OR08)

- apply the Plans component to a given project scenario (PL08)

- produce any of the products of Configuration Management in a given project scenario (CM10).

Level 4: Analysis

Analysis refers to the ability to break down material into its component parts so that its organisational structure may be understood. This may include the identification of parts, analysis of the relationship between parts, and recognition of the underlying principles involved. Learning outcomes here represent a higher intellectual level than comprehension and application because they require an understanding of both the content and the structural form of the material.

For the Practitioner this maps to the competency to **analyse the use of the method.** This is not the ability to use analysis techniques such as risk analysis and product-based planning – these are tested as an application competency. Typically competency would test the ability to identify errors with the application of PRINCE2 or to identify the aspects of a PRINCE2 component or technique that could be of benefit in a given project situation. To answer these kinds of question candidates must have breadth of understanding of the topic, understand how that component/process/technique interacts with other components/processes/techniques and the implications of this for a given project scenario.

Examples of syllabus topics that match this learning level are:

- understand the relationship between Controls and other PRINCE2 components within any given project scenario (CO17)

- understand the relationship between Change Controls and other PRINCE2 components within any given project scenario (CC15).

N.B. The 'discuss' test usually combines 'analysis' with the next learning level 'evaluate' – 'analysis' being the ability to identify the weaknesses or problems and 'evaluate' to explain why the points identified are 'weaknesses'.

Level 5: Synthesis

This refers to the ability to put parts together to form a new whole. Learning outcomes in this area stress creative behaviours, with major emphasis on the formulation of new patterns or structure.

Creation of a project's PRINCE2 products is an inherent part of application of the method and is tested as an Application competency. Synthesis best maps to the understanding and creativity required to design and modify a PRINCE2 implementation at organisational level. This competency is not tested in the Practitioner Examination and has been excluded from the Practitioner learning objectives.

Level 6: Evaluation

Evaluation is concerned with the ability to judge the value of something for a given purpose. Learning outcomes in this area are highest in the cognitive hierarchy because they contain elements of all the other categories plus conscious value judgements.

This maps to the ability of a Practitioner candidate to evaluate or justify the use of the method in a given project situation. It is closely linked to the analysis competency but builds on this by requiring the candidate to explain or justify the recommendations they have made and maps to the syllabus statements 'explain the reasons', 'discuss the use of' and 'justify the use of'. The distinction is useful as we have seen in the essay exam that candidates are often able to recognise weaknesses in a document but cannot explain why the weakness is a problem.

Examples of syllabus topics that match this learning level are:

- modify or discuss the use of any level of plan for any given project scenario (PL07)

- modify or discuss a project organisation from information provided in a given project scenario (OR12)

- justify the use of PRINCE2 to a given scenario and explain the benefits of its application to that scenario (OV08).

The syllabus

Syllabus reference		Syllabus area	Foundation	Practitioner	Level
Overview and principles					
OV	01	Know the typical characteristics of a project.	✓	✓	1
OV	02	Know the benefits of a structured approach to project management.	✓	✓	1
OV	03	Understand the relationship between the project environment and the daily business of an organisation.	✓	✓	2
OV	04	Understand the differences between the project lifecycle and the product lifespan.	✓	✓	2
OV	05	Know what part of a product lifespan is covered by PRINCE2.	✓	✓	1
OV	06	Know the main elements of PRINCE2, including the eight processes, the components and the techniques.	✓	✓	1
OV	07	Understand PRINCE2 terminology, including customer, supplier, user, product, Business Case, exception and stage.	✓	✓	2
OV	08	Justify the use of PRINCE2 for a given project scenario, and explain the benefits of its application to that scenario.		✓	6

Overview and principles will not be treated as a separate section of the objective setting Practitioner paper, but questions at overview or principles level will be included in each of the other syllabus areas.

			Foundation	Practitioner	Level
Organisation					
OR	01	Know the purpose of organisation.	✓	✓	1
OR	02	Understand the principles and benefits of the PRINCE2 project management structure.		✓	2
OR	03	Know the four layers in the project organisation structure, including the differences between the management and the direction of a project.	✓	✓	1
OR	04	Understand the differing business, user and supplier interests of participating parties in a project, and how these will be represented within the standard project organisation structure, and understand the acceptable consolidations or sharing of roles.	✓	✓	2
OR	05	Know the products of organisation.	✓	✓	1
OR	06	Understand the purpose and responsibilities of the Project Board, Project Manager, Project Assurance, Team Manager and Project Support.	✓	✓	2
OR	07	Understand the contributions of the Project Assurance roles in the various processes.		✓	2

Syllabus reference		Syllabus area	Foundation	Practitioner	Level
OR	08	Design an appropriate project organisation, applying all roles as identified in PRINCE2, and explain the responsibilities of each role for a given project scenario.		✓	3
OR	09	Apply and explain acceptable role consolidations or sharing and their resulting organisation structure to a given project scenario.		✓	3
OR	10	Produce role descriptions for the Project Board, Project Manager, Team Manager, Project Assurance and Project Support, tuned for the particular needs of a given project scenario.		✓	3
OR	11	Understand the relationship between organisation and other PRINCE2 components within a given project scenario.		✓	4
OR	12	Modify or discuss a project organisation from information provided in a given project scenario.		✓	6

Business Case

			Foundation	Practitioner	Level
BN	01	Understand the importance of the benefits focus of PRINCE2 in project management.	✓	✓	2
BN	02	Know the purpose of the Business Case.	✓	✓	1
BN	03	Understand the principles behind the Business Case and the benefits of using it.	✓	✓	2
BN	04	Understand the contents of a Business Case, in which process(es) it is produced, monitored and updated, and which roles are responsible for this work.		✓	2
BN	05	Understand the factors in a project that would be considered in the development of the Business Case.		✓	2
BN	06	Understand how a Business Case would be produced, updated, used and modified within the PRINCE2 processes, and how the various roles would be involved, by application to a given project scenario.		✓	3
BN	07	Produce a Business Case from information provided in a given project scenario.		✓	3
BN	08	Modify or discuss a Business Case from information provided in a given project scenario.		✓	6
BN	09	Understand the relationship between the Business Case and other PRINCE2 products and components in any given project scenario.		✓	4
BN	10	State benefits in measurable terms for a given project scenario.		✓	3

Knowledge of the Business Case contents excludes any detailed knowledge of how to perform an Investment Appraisal or techniques such as sensitivity analysis and GAP analysis.

Syllabus reference		Syllabus area	Foundation	Practitioner	Level

Controls

CO	01	Know the purpose of Controls.	✓	✓	1
CO	02	Understand the principles and benefits of Controls.		✓	2
CO	03	Know the products involved in the controlled start of a project.	✓	✓	1
CO	04	Understand the purpose and contents of each product involved in the controlled start of a project.		✓	2
CO	05	Know the products used to manage the controlled progress of a project.	✓	✓	1
CO	06	Understand the purpose and content of each product used to manage the controlled progress of a project.		✓	2
CO	07	Understand the purpose, types and application of tolerance.	✓	✓	2
CO	08	Understand the reasons for breaking a project into stages and understand the difference between management and technical stages.	✓	✓	2
CO	09	Know the products involved in bringing a project to a controlled close.	✓	✓	1
CO	10	Understand the purpose and contents of each product involved in bringing a project to a controlled close.		✓	2
CO	11	Understand the responsibilities of Controls and activities of the various PRINCE2 roles within each of the eight processes.	✓	✓	2
CO	12	Produce any of the products of Controls in a given project scenario.		✓	3
CO	13	Modify or discuss any of the products of Controls in a given project scenario.		✓	6
CO	14	Understand each Control, its purpose and content, the relevant processes involved in its application, and which roles are involved.		✓	2
CO	15	Understand the reporting and information flow relationships between roles.		✓	2
CO	16	Apply any of the Controls defined by PRINCE2 to a given project scenario.		✓	3
CO	17	Understand the relationship between Controls and other PRINCE2 components within any given project scenario.		✓	4

Change Control and Change Control Approach

CC	01	Know the purpose of Change Control.	✓	✓	1
CC	02	Understand the principles and benefits of Change Control.	✓	✓	2
CC	03	Know the products of Change Control.	✓	✓	1
CC	04	Understand the content and purpose of a Project Issue, Request for Change and Off-Specification.		✓	2
CC	05	Understand the link between Change Control and Configuration Management.	✓	✓	2
CC	06	Understand the PRINCE2 Change Control Approach technique.	✓	✓	2

Syllabus reference		Syllabus area	Foundation	Practitioner	Level
CC	07	Understand the Change Control responsibilities and activities of the various PRINCE2 roles within each of the eight processes.	✓	✓	2
CC	08	Produce the products of Change Control for a given project scenario.		✓	3
CC	09	Modify or discuss the products of Change Control for a given project scenario.		✓	6
CC	10	Apply the Change Control Approach technique to a given project scenario.		✓	3
CC	11	Understand the factors determining escalation of Project Issues to the Project Manager, Project Board and senior management, and the processes involved.		✓	2
CC	12	Produce any of the products required in escalation of Project Issues to the Project Board for a given project scenario.		✓	3
CC	13	Modify or discuss any of the products required in escalation of Project Issues to the Project Board for a given project scenario.		✓	6
CC	14	Understand the factors affecting the application of the Change Budget and the appointment of a Change Authority in any given project scenario.		✓	3
CC	15	Understand the relationship between Change Control and other PRINCE2 components within a given project scenario.		✓	4

Management of Risk

			Foundation	Practitioner	Level
RK	01	Know the purpose of Management of Risk.	✓	✓	1
RK	02	Understand the principles and benefits of Management of Risk, and explain the PRINCE2 risk management cycle.	✓	✓	2
RK	03	Understand the purpose of the Risk Log, in which process(es) it is produced, monitored and updated, and the main responsibilities of the PRINCE2 roles for risk, including the concept of risk owner.	✓	✓	2
RK	04	Understand the concept of risk tolerance.	✓	✓	2
RK	05	Apply Management of Risk (i.e. risk analysis and risk management) to a given project scenario.		✓	3
RK	06	Assess the interdependencies and potential impact between the various risk areas.		✓	3
RK	07	Produce a Risk Log for a given project scenario.		✓	3
RK	08	Modify or discuss a Risk Log for a given project scenario.		✓	6
RK	09	Understand the relationship between Management of Risk and other PRINCE2 components in a given project scenario.		✓	4

Syllabus reference		Syllabus area	Foundation	Practitioner	Level
Quality in a project environment					
QU	01	Know the purpose of quality management.	✓	✓	1
QU	02	Understand the benefits of and principles behind quality management.	✓	✓	2
QU	03	Know the products of quality management.	✓	✓	1
QU	04	Understand the purpose and content of each product of quality management.		✓	2
QU	05	Understand the importance of the customer's quality expectations.	✓	✓	2
QU	06	Understand the part played by a quality management system from the user or supplier in contributing to a Project Quality Plan.	✓	✓	2
QU	07	Understand the quality management responsibilities and activities of the various PRINCE2 roles within the processes.	✓	✓	2
QU	08	Understand the PRINCE2 quality path through a project.	✓	✓	2
QU	09	Understand the relationship between a quality assurance function and the Project Assurance role.	✓	✓	2
QU	10	Understand the role played by Project Assurance in the PRINCE2 processes, components and techniques.		✓	2
QU	11	Produce any of the products of quality management in a given project scenario.		✓	3
QU	12	Modify or discuss any of the products of quality management in a given project scenario.		✓	6
QU	13	Apply quality management to a given project scenario.		✓	3
QU	14	Understand the relationship between quality management and other PRINCE2 components within a given project scenario.		✓	4

Candidates are not required to have any detailed understanding of ISO 9000:2000.

Plans					
PL	01	Know the purpose of the Plans component.		✓	1
PL	02	Understand the principles and benefits of the Plans component.		✓	2
PL	03	Understand the responsibilities for Plans and activities of the PRINCE2 roles within the processes.		✓	2
PL	04	Understand the purpose and content of the Project Plan, Stage Plans, Team Plans and Exception Plan, and in which process(es) these plans are produced, monitored and updated.		✓	2
PL	05	Understand the inter-relationship between the Project Plan, Stage Plans, Team Plans and an Exception Plan.		✓	2

Syllabus reference		Syllabus area	Foundation	Practitioner	Level
PL	06	Produce any level of plan for a given project scenario.		✓	3
PL	07	Modify or discuss any level of plan for a given project scenario.		✓	6
PL	08	Apply the Plans component to a given project scenario.		✓	3
PL	09	Understand the relationship between Plans and other PRINCE2 components within a given project scenario.		✓	4

Required knowledge of the techniques of network planning and Gantt charts reaches only as far as being able to know the PRINCE2 processes in which they might be produced, and does not include how to produce/modify or use these techniques (Practitioner level only).

Configuration Management

			Foundation	Practitioner	Level
CM	01	Know the purpose of Configuration Management.	✓	✓	1
CM	02	Understand the principles and benefits of Configuration Management.	✓	✓	2
CM	03	Understand version control and the reasons for it.	✓	✓	2
CM	04	Know the products of Configuration Management.	✓	✓	1
CM	05	Understand the PRINCE2 filing structure.	✓	✓	2
CM	06	Understand the Configuration Management responsibilities and activities of the various PRINCE2 roles within each of the eight processes.	✓	✓	2
CM	07	Understand the Configuration Librarian role, and the relationship of this role to all the other PRINCE2 defined roles.	✓	✓	2
CM	08	Understand the relationship between Configuration Management and Change Control.	✓	✓	2
CM	09	Understand the relationship between project Configuration Management and operational Configuration Management.	✓	✓	2
CM	10	Produce any of the products of Configuration Management in a given project scenario.		✓	3
CM	11	Modify or discuss any of the products of Configuration Management in a given project scenario.		✓	6
CM	12	Apply Configuration Management to a given project scenario.		✓	3
CM	13	Understand how to integrate the requirements of project Configuration Management with an existing operational Configuration Management environment for a given project scenario.		✓	6
CM	14	Understand the relationship between Configuration Management and other PRINCE2 components within a given project scenario.		✓	4

Syllabus reference		Syllabus area	Foundation	Practitioner	Level
Processes					
PR	01	Know the purpose, inputs and outputs of each of the eight processes, and their normal sequence.	✓	✓	1
PR	02	Understand the objectives, inputs and outputs of each of the sub-processes of Controlling a Stage (CS) and Managing Product Delivery (MP), and their normal sequence.	✓		
PR	03	Understand the objectives, inputs and outputs for all of the processes and the main steps involved in the carrying out of each of the processes as described by PRINCE2.	✓	✓	2
PR	04	Apply the processes of PRINCE2 to a given project scenario.		✓	3
PR	05	Discuss the application of the PRINCE2 processes, their interfaces and interdependencies in a given project scenario.		✓	6
PR	06	Understand the responsibilities of each PRINCE2 role in each of the processes.		✓	2
PR	07	Understand the passage of all PRINCE2 products through the processes.		✓	2

The Practitioner Examination will test at process level, not at a detailed level of sub-processes.

Syllabus reference		Syllabus area	Foundation	Practitioner	Level
Product-based planning					
PP	01	Understand the steps involved in product-based planning.	✓	✓	2
PP	02	Understand the principles and benefits of product-based planning.	✓	✓	2
PP	03	Understand where in the processes product-based planning is used.	✓	✓	2
PP	04	Know the purpose of the three PRINCE2 product-based planning products.	✓	✓	1
PP	05	Understand the content of the three product-based planning products, and which PRINCE2 roles should be involved in their production and use.		✓	2
PP	06	Produce a Product Breakdown Structure and Product Flow Diagram for a given project scenario.		✓	3
PP	07	Modify or discuss a Product Breakdown Structure and Product Flow Diagram for a given project scenario.		✓	6
PP	08	Produce a Product Description for a product identified in a given project scenario.		✓	3
PP	09	Modify or discuss a Product Description for a product identified in a given project scenario.		✓	6
PP	10	Understand the difference in intermediate products between integration products and collective groupings.		✓	2

Syllabus reference		Syllabus area	Foundation	Practitioner	Level
PP	11	Understand the difference between external products and project products produced by external suppliers for a given scenario.		✓	3

Quality Review

QR	01	Know the purpose of a Quality Review.	✓	✓	1
QR	02	Understand the principles and benefits of a Quality Review.	✓	✓	2
QR	03	Know the three steps of a Quality Review.	✓	✓	1
QR	04	Understand the purpose and content of the products used in a Quality Review.	✓	✓	2
QR	05	Understand where within the PRINCE2 processes Quality Reviews are planned and conducted, and how the various roles of the project management team are involved in their planning and conduct.	✓	✓	2
QR	06	Understand the roles used in a Quality Review, and how these relate to the standard PRINCE2 roles.	✓	✓	2
QR	07	Produce any of the products of a Quality Review in a given project scenario.		✓	3
QR	08	Modify or discuss any of the products of a Quality Review in a given project scenario.		✓	6
QR	09	Apply the Quality Review technique to a given project scenario.		✓	3
QR	10	Understand the links between a Quality Review, the processes and project management team roles for a given project scenario.		✓	4

The Foundation Examination

What is the examination?

The Foundation Examination is a one-hour, closed-book examination. It is designed to test the candidate's knowledge of the PRINCE2 method by providing them with a selection of possible answers from which they must select the correct one. There are 75 questions in all and candidates must score 38 correct answers or more to pass. There is no consolidation or carry-forward of time or scores to the Practitioner Examination – the Foundation Examination stands alone. Candidates intending to take the PRINCE2 Practitioner Examination (or any other PRINCE-related examination) must first pass the Foundation Examination.

The track record

Statistics released by the APM Group to PRINCE2 Accredited Training Organisations (ATOs) show that around 95% of all candidates pass the Foundation Examination, indicating that the level of understanding of the PRINCE2 terminology and overview of the method is high.

The Practitioner Examination requires candidates to demonstrate that they are able to apply the method to a project situation. Only around 65% of candidates taking the Registered Practitioner Examination reach the required standard, indicating that the examination is quite a tough test of their ability to answer objective testing questions on the PRINCE2 method. A later section of this publication provides advice and guidance on the Practitioner Examination.

There is an interesting correlation between marks scored in the Foundation Examination and success in the Practitioner Examination – essentially the more marks scored in the Foundation Examination, the higher the success rate at practitioner level. Candidates who pass the Foundation Examination with 38–40 marks are, statistically, much less likely to pass the Practitioner Examination; those with Foundation Examination scores in excess of 70 marks almost always pass the Practitioner Examination.

The examination questions

On the following pages are examples of the questions and multiple-choice answers that make up the Foundation Examination. Do not approach the questions 'cold'; you must have done quite a bit of preparation before attempting any, otherwise you will get demoralised!

There are over 450 questions in the APM Group database from which the actual examination questions are taken. Some of the questions are very straightforward and will give you little trouble; others drill down into the method and are there to really test your knowledge. You will find that some of the possible answers posed can be eliminated with even a basic knowledge of the method.

Preparing for the examination

Success in the Foundation Examination requires a good understanding of PRINCE2 terminology, an overview of the method and the flows of information within it. The official OGC PRINCE2 manual (*Managing Successful Projects with PRINCE2* ISBN: 978 0 11 330946 7) does not contain a single, overall, detailed process map and it is well worth studying the one shown in Figure 2 as part of your preparation for the examination.

Figure 2 takes each of the major processes and maps the flows of information and products between them.

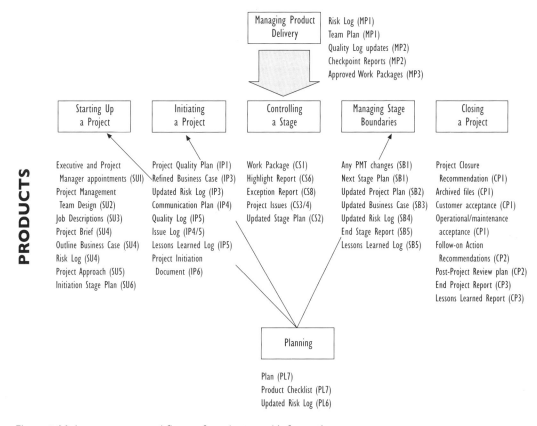

Figure 2 Major processes, and flows of products and information

The acronym in brackets after each product identifies the sub-process that creates it. Remember, for the Foundation Examination, you do not need to go down to the sub-process level in most processes, only in the Controlling a Stage (CS) and Managing Product Delivery (MP) processes. As part of your preparation, try to produce your own diagram – do not simply rely on the one shown here!

Remember that the main benefit from creating your own summary process diagram will come from the research you will need to do into each process. You will not be allowed to take your summary process diagram into the Foundation Examination, but it will be a useful revision aid.

Technique for completing the examination

The paper contains 75 questions, most of which offer four possible answers. Occasionally there will be only two options, e.g. TRUE or FALSE. One (and only one) of the options will be the correct answer. All you have to do is put a tick or cross in the box that corresponds to your chosen answer for that question on the appropriate row on the answer sheet that is provided.

The best technique for the Foundation Examination is to go through the paper in a first non-stop 'sweep', answering all the straightforward questions to which you know the answers; ignore any long, wordy questions or those that might need some working out. The paper may include 'negative' questions (i.e. *'Which of the following options is FALSE ...'*) and you might find it easier to return to these at a later time.

When your first sweep is completed you should have most of the questions answered; typically this will take about 15–25 minutes. You can at this stage count up the number of questions you know you have answered correctly to provide a confidence boost – but beware that this might have the opposite effect!

Now return to those more obscure or difficult questions in a second sweep. Many will not be as tricky as they first appeared and, with a bit of common sense and careful reading of the question, you should be able to discount many of the options offered. This may leave you with one option that on re-examination is clearly the correct option. For other questions, you may be left with, say, two options from which you still cannot choose. Leave these and continue the second sweep. You should now feel confident that you are well beyond the pass mark and still have time to spare. Return for a third sweep through those (few) outstanding questions. Review the question and the remaining options. For some, the answer may now suggest itself. For the others, think about them again, but before time runs out, at least make a guess. You should have at least a fifty-fifty chance of being right.

Beware of changing answers you have already made – general experience indicates that there are probably as many changes made from correct to incorrect answers as there are from incorrect to correct! If you need to make a change, show it clearly.

You should now be ready to try a Foundation Examination paper – if you have done your preparation work you should be feeling quite confident and ready to tackle the example examination which starts on the next page. Always plan your approach to the real examination – time the completion of the example paper that follows for no more than two days before the examination – you will then be finely honed – with just enough time to review the elements you missed out on but not too much time to cause you to lose the cutting edge you'll need for the real thing.

Good luck!

Sample Foundation Examination Paper

Multiple Choice

Instructions

1	All 75 questions should be attempted.
2	There are no trick questions.
3	All answers are to be marked on the original examination paper.
4	Please use a pen to mark your answers with either a ✓ or ✗.
5	You have 1 hour for this paper.
6	You must get 38 or more correct to pass.

Candidate Number: ....

1.   In PRINCE2 what product is used to define the information that justifies the setting up, continuation or termination of the project?

     a)   Project Initiation Document   ☐

     b)   Business Case   ☐

     c)   End Stage Approval   ☐

     d)   Project Brief   ☐

2.   Which product keeps track of Requests for Change?

     a)   Request Log   ☐

     b)   Daily Log   ☐

     c)   Quality Log   ☐

     d)   Issue Log   ☐

3.   What provision in Planning can be made for implementing Requests for Change?

     a)   Project and stage tolerances   ☐

     b)   Contingency plans   ☐

     c)   A Change Budget   ☐

     d)   Adding a contingency margin to estimates   ☐

4.   Fill in the missing phrase from 'a project is a management environment that is created for the purpose of delivering one or more business products according to …'

     a)   the Customer's Needs   ☐

     b)   an Agreed Contract   ☐

     c)   the Project Plan   ☐

     d)   a specified Business Case   ☐

5.   In what sequence would (a) the Project Initiation Document, (b) the Project Mandate and (c) the Project Brief appear in a PRINCE2 project?

     a)   a, b, c   ☐

     b)   b, c, a   ☐

     c)   c, a, b   ☐

     d)   c, b, a   ☐

6.   Which would require the production of an Exception Report?

    a)   When a Project Issue is received ☐

    b)   When a Project Board member raises a complaint ☐

    c)   When a Request for Change or Off-Specification has been received ☐

    d)   When the current forecasts for the end of the stage deviate beyond the delegated tolerance bounds ☐

7.   Which statement is NOT a fundamental principle of 'Closing a Project'?

    'A clear end to a project ...'

    a)   provides a useful opportunity to take stock of achievements ☐

    b)   provides an opportunity to ensure that all unachieved goals and objectives are identified ☐

    c)   provides the opportunity to evaluate achievement of all the expected benefits ☐

    d)   is always more successful than the natural tendency to drift into operational management ☐

8.   What is the more common term used in PRINCE2 for 'deliverable'?

    a)   Item ☐

    b)   Package ☐

    c)   Product ☐

    d)   Component ☐

9.   Which of these items does NOT involve the Project Board?

    a)   Exception Assessment ☐

    b)   Highlight Reports ☐

    c)   Project Closure ☐

    d)   Work Package Authorisation ☐

10.   What name is given to the permissible deviation from a plan allowed without immediate reporting to the Project Board?

   a)   Allowance

   b)   Contingency

   c)   Concession

   d)   Tolerance

11.   What other control is closely linked with Configuration Management?

   a)   Risk Management

   b)   Project Closure

   c)   Change Control

   d)   Project Initiation

12.   Which of these processes does NOT trigger the Planning (PL) process?

   a)   Starting Up a Project (SU)

   b)   Initiating a Project (IP)

   c)   Managing Stage Boundaries (SB)

   d)   Controlling a Stage (CS)

13.   In a Product Breakdown Structure what category of product is a Highlight Report?

   a)   Quality

   b)   Specialist

   c)   Technical

   d)   Management

14.   If, after a Quality Review Follow-up Action, an error is still not resolved, what action should be taken?

   a)   An Exception Report is made

   b)   A Project Issue is raised

   c)   An Exception Memo is raised

   d)   The review is reconvened

15. Which of the following is NOT a PRINCE2 definition of a project?

    a) Has an organisation structure ☐

    b) Produces defined and measurable business products ☐

    c) Uses a defined amount of resources ☐

    d) Uses a defined set of techniques ☐

16. What environment does PRINCE2 assume?

    a) A fixed-price contract ☐

    b) A customer/supplier environment ☐

    c) A specialist environment ☐

    d) A third-party environment ☐

17. Which feature of PRINCE2 tells the Project Manager where a product is, what its status is and who is working on it?

    a) Work Package ☐

    b) Product Description ☐

    c) Checkpoint Report ☐

    d) Configuration Management ☐

18. In 'Closing a Project' (CP) the project files are archived. What is the explanation given for this?

    a) To provide useful lessons to future projects ☐

    b) Never throw anything away ☐

    c) This material may be needed by Programme Management ☐

    d) To permit any future audit of the project's actions ☐

19. Which of the following statements is FALSE? Project Managers using PRINCE2 are encouraged to …

    a) establish terms of reference as a prerequisite to the start of the project ☐

    b) use a defined structure for delegation, authority and communication ☐

    c) divide the project into manageable stages for more accurate planning ☐

    d) provide brief reports to Management at regular meetings ☐

20.   Which of these is NOT a valid Risk Management action?

    a)   Prevention   ☐

    b)   Denial   ☐

    c)   Reduction   ☐

    d)   Transference   ☐

21.   Which one of these is NOT a PRINCE2 component?

    a)   Plans   ☐

    b)   Controls   ☐

    c)   Work Package   ☐

    d)   Configuration Management   ☐

22.   Which document lists the major products of a plan with their key delivery dates?

    a)   Product Outline   ☐

    b)   Product Breakdown Structure   ☐

    c)   Checkpoint Report   ☐

    d)   Product Checklist   ☐

23.   The configuration of the final deliverable of the project is:

    a)   the sum total of its products   ☐

    b)   the interim products   ☐

    c)   its Product Description   ☐

    d)   the single end-product   ☐

24.   Which part of a product lifespan is not part of a project lifecycle in the eyes of PRINCE2?

    a)   The change-over to operational use of the product   ☐

    b)   Assessment of the value of the product after a period of use   ☐

    c)   The specification of the product   ☐

    d)   Finalisation of the Business Case   ☐

25.   What is the first job carried out on receipt of a new Project Issue?

    a)   Allocation of priority ☐

    b)   Logging ☐

    c)   Decision on what type of issue ☐

    d)   Impact Analysis ☐

26.   Which of these statements is FALSE?

    a)   The Project Plan is an overview of the total project ☐

    b)   For each stage identified in the Project Plan, a Stage Plan is required ☐

    c)   An Exception Plan needs the approval of the next higher level of authority ☐

    d)   A Team Plan needs approval by the Project Board ☐

27.   Which of the following statements is FALSE?

    a)   Customer quality expectations should be discovered in the process 'Starting Up a Project' ☐

    b)   A company's QMS becomes part of PRINCE2 ☐

    c)   PRINCE2 may form part of a company's QMS ☐

    d)   The Stage Plan describes in detail how part of the Project Plan will be carried out ☐

28.   Which one of these statements describes the true purpose of Acceptance Criteria?

    a)   A justification for undertaking the project based on estimated costs and anticipated benefits ☐

    b)   A measurable definition of what must be done for the final product to be acceptable to the customer ☐

    c)   To provide a full and firm foundation for the initiation of a project ☐

    d)   To trigger 'Starting Up a Project' ☐

29.   How often does PRINCE2 recommend that open Project Issues should be reviewed?

    a)   Weekly ☐

    b)   At Exception Assessments ☐

    c)   At Checkpoint Meetings ☐

    d)   On a regular basis ☐

30. What other product is reviewed at the end of each stage apart from the Business Case and Project Plan?

    a)   The Project Mandate ☐

    b)   The Quality Log ☐

    c)   The Risk Log ☐

    d)   The Project Brief ☐

31. Why is a copy of the Project Issue always returned to the author?

    a)   The author owns it ☐

    b)   To acknowledge its receipt and entry into the system ☐

    c)   To elicit further information ☐

    d)   To notify rejection of the Issue ☐

32. Which product reviews the benefits achieved by the project?

    a)   Post-Project Review ☐

    b)   Post-Project Review Plan ☐

    c)   End Project Report ☐

    d)   Follow-on Action Recommendations ☐

33. Which of these statements is FALSE?

    a)   A PRINCE2 project has a finite lifespan ☐

    b)   A PRINCE2 project has a defined amount of resources ☐

    c)   A PRINCE2 project may have only activities, i.e. no products ☐

    d)   A PRINCE2 project has an organisation structure with defined responsibilities to manage the project ☐

34. The person best situated to keep an eye on a risk is called its … ?

    a)   Supporter ☐

    b)   Monitor ☐

    c)   Owner ☐

    d)   Librarian ☐

35. Which document reviews actual achievements against the Project Initiation Document?

     a)   End Project Report   ☐

     b)   Post-Project Review   ☐

     c)   Lessons Learned Report   ☐

     d)   Follow-on Action Recommendations   ☐

36. In PRINCE2 all potential changes are dealt with as ...?

     a)   Configuration Items   ☐

     b)   Requests for Change   ☐

     c)   Project Issues   ☐

     d)   Exception Reports   ☐

     e)   Action items   ☐

37. Which one of these is NOT a key criterion for producing a Product Flow Diagram?

     a)   Are the products clearly and unambiguously defined?   ☐

     b)   On what other products is each product dependent?   ☐

     c)   Is any product dependent on a product outside the scope of this plan?   ☐

     d)   Which products can be developed in parallel?   ☐

38. For a Quality Review, when are suitable reviewers identified?

     a)   When the product is passed to Configuration Management   ☐

     b)   In the Project Quality Plan   ☐

     c)   During the QR preparation step   ☐

     d)   In planning the relevant stage   ☐

39. The existence of what product is checked in 'Starting Up a Project' and its initial version finalised in 'Initiating a Project'?

     a)   The Project Mandate   ☐

     b)   The Project Plan   ☐

     c)   The Project Brief   ☐

     d)   The Business Case   ☐

40. Which does PRINCE2 regard as the third project interest, given user and supplier as the other two?

   a)   Technical ☐

   b)   Management ☐

   c)   Business ☐

   d)   Quality ☐

41. PRINCE2 lists a number of reasons why it is seldom desirable or possible to plan an entire project in detail at the start. Which of these is NOT one of these reasons?

   a)   A changing or uncertain environment ☐

   b)   A PRINCE2 requirement ☐

   c)   Difficulty in predicting business conditions in the future ☐

   d)   Difficulty in predicting resource availability well into the future ☐

42. In which process is the Project Brief produced?

   a)   Starting Up a Project ☐

   b)   Initiating a Project ☐

   c)   Authorising Initiation ☐

   d)   Authorising a Project ☐

43. When should a Product Description be baselined?

   a)   As soon as it is available in draft form ☐

   b)   When the associated product has passed its quality check ☐

   c)   When the plan containing its creation is baselined ☐

   d)   As soon as it is written ☐

44. An Exception Plan covers what period?

   a)   From the problem to the end of the project ☐

   b)   From the problem to the end of a plan that will no longer finish within agreed tolerances ☐

   c)   The work needed to put the project back within its tolerances ☐

   d)   The time needed to produce an Exception Report ☐

45. Stage boundaries may be chosen according to a number of parameters. Which one of the following is NOT one of the parameters?

   a) The need to have a separate stage for the formal close of the project ☐

   b) A review of a risky project at key moments when new information about those risks appears ☐

   c) Ensuring that key decisions are made prior to the detailed work needed to implement them ☐

   d) Providing a 'fire break' for the project by encouraging the Project Board to assess the project viability at regular intervals ☐

46. The initial Project Plan is based on the Project Brief, the Project Quality Plan and which other product?

   a) The Project Approach ☐

   b) The Project Initiation Document ☐

   c) The project start-up notification ☐

   d) The Project Mandate ☐

47. Which document is a record of some current or forecast failure to meet a requirement?

   a) Exception Report ☐

   b) Off-Specification ☐

   c) Follow-on Action Recommendations ☐

   d) Highlight Report ☐

48. If there is a request to change a baselined product, and the change can be done within the stage or Work Package tolerances, how can the decision to implement the change be made?

   a) Project Manager's decision ☐

   b) Team Manager's decision ☐

   c) Team member's decision to whom the work has been allocated ☐

   d) Formal Change Control ☐

49.   'Controlling a Stage' drives which other process on a frequent, iterative basis?

      a)   Managing Stage Boundaries   □

      b)   Approving a Stage or Exception Plan   □

      c)   Managing Product Delivery   □

      d)   Planning   □

50.   The Project Quality Plan is written in which process?

      a)   Initiating a Project   □

      b)   Starting Up a Project   □

      c)   Managing Stage Boundaries   □

      d)   Directing a Project   □

51.   What are defined as 'partitions of the project with decision points'?

      a)   Work Packages   □

      b)   Product Descriptions   □

      c)   Quality Reviews   □

      d)   Stages   □

52.   In which lower-level process of 'Controlling a Stage' is the Risk Log updated?

      a)   Reporting Highlights   □

      b)   Assessing Progress   □

      c)   Capturing Project Issues   □

      d)   Examining Project Issues   □

53.   If a question arises on why a particular product was changed, which element of PRINCE2 would be of most help in finding the information?

      a)   Issue Log   □

      b)   Quality Log   □

      c)   Configuration Management   □

      d)   Change Control   □

54. In which sub-process is a Stage Plan updated with actuals?

   a)   Assessing Progress   ☐

   b)   Reviewing Stage Status   ☐

   c)   Planning a Stage   ☐

   d)   Reporting Highlights   ☐

55. In which sub-process are Checkpoint Reports created?

   a)   Executing a Work Package   ☐

   b)   Assessing Progress   ☐

   c)   Reporting Highlights   ☐

   d)   Reviewing Stage Status   ☐

56. Are the following statements true or false?

   –   Delegated Project Assurance roles report directly to corporate or programme management

   –   In PRINCE2 the Project Manager role must be full time

   –   A project management structure is a temporary structure

   a)   All three are false   ☐

   b)   Only the third is true   ☐

   c)   Only the first is false   ☐

   d)   The second and third are false   ☐

57. The process, 'Directing a Project' begins when?

   a)   From 'Starting Up a Project'   ☐

   b)   After the start-up of the project   ☐

   c)   At the end of the Initiation Stage   ☐

   d)   Before start-up of the project   ☐

58. Apart from 'Initiating a Project', in which process is the Business Case updated?

   a)   Managing Product Delivery   ☐

   b)   Controlling a Stage   ☐

   c)   Managing Stage Boundaries   ☐

   d)   Authorising a Stage   ☐

59.   The existence of what information is expected by the process 'Starting Up a Project'?

    a)   A Project Plan ☐

    b)   A Project Mandate ☐

    c)   An appointed organisation ☐

    d)   Project Initiation Document ☐

60.   In the PRINCE2 document management structure, how many types of file are recommended?

    a)   One for each Stage ☐

    b)   Two; Management and Specialist ☐

    c)   Just the Quality File ☐

    d)   Three; Project, Stages and Quality ☐

61.   In a Quality Review which role does PRINCE2 suggest must ensure that all reviewers are provided with the relevant review products?

    a)   Producer ☐

    b)   Scribe ☐

    c)   Review Chairperson ☐

    d)   Configuration Librarian ☐

62.   Which of these is mandatory in a PRINCE2 project?

    a)   The use of Team Managers ☐

    b)   The use of Exception Plans ☐

    c)   The use of Stages ☐

    d)   The use of Quality Reviews ☐

63.   The Project Board has three responsibilities towards the Management of Risk. Which of the following options is the FALSE one?

    a)   Notifying the Project Manager of any external risk exposure to the project ☐

    b)   Making decisions on recommended reactions to risk ☐

    c)   Identifying, recording and regularly reviewing risks ☐

    d)   Striking a balance between levels of risk and potential benefits ☐

64.　　What function creates, maintains and monitors the use of a quality system?

　　　a)　　Project Support　　☐

　　　b)　　Quality Planning　　☐

　　　c)　　Quality Control　　☐

　　　d)　　Quality assurance　　☐

65.　　Which is not a purpose of Configuration Management?

　　　a)　　To identify products　　☐

　　　b)　　To create products　　☐

　　　c)　　To track products　　☐

　　　d)　　To protect products　　☐

66.　　Which step is NOT part of 'Accepting a Work Package'?

　　　a)　　Understand the reporting requirements　　☐

　　　b)　　Agree tolerance margins for the Work Package　　☐

　　　c)　　Monitor and control the risks associated with the Work Package　　☐

　　　d)　　Produce a Team Plan which shows that the Work Package can be completed within the constraints　　☐

67.　　Which process provides the information needed for the Project Board to assess the continuing viability of the project?

　　　a)　　Starting Up a Project　　☐

　　　b)　　Closing a Project　　☐

　　　c)　　Planning　　☐

　　　d)　　Managing Stage Boundaries　　☐

68.　　In which process are choices made about planning tools and estimating methods?

　　　a)　　Starting Up a Project　　☐

　　　b)　　Initiating a Project　　☐

　　　c)　　Managing Stage Boundaries　　☐

　　　d)　　Planning　　☐

69.   In which process are decisions made on Exception Reports?

     a)   Managing Stage Boundaries   ☐

     b)   Closing a Project   ☐

     c)   Directing a Project   ☐

     d)   Managing Product Delivery   ☐

70.   Which process checks for changes to the project management team?

     a)   Starting Up a Project   ☐

     b)   Managing Stage Boundaries   ☐

     c)   Closing a Project   ☐

     d)   Directing a Project   ☐

71.   From the products listed, which one is produced during 'Starting Up a Project'?

     a)   The Project Initiation Document   ☐

     b)   The Project Plan   ☐

     c)   The Project Quality Plan   ☐

     d)   The Project Approach   ☐

72.   Quality responsibilities, both within and external to the project, are defined in which process?

     a)   Initiating a Project   ☐

     b)   Starting Up a Project   ☐

     c)   Managing Stage Boundaries   ☐

     d)   Directing a Project   ☐

73.   Acceptance for the completed products is obtained as part of which process?

     a)   Closing a Project   ☐

     b)   Managing Product Delivery   ☐

     c)   Managing Stage Boundaries   ☐

     d)   Controlling a Stage   ☐

74.   An Exception Report is produced in which sub-process?

    a)   Taking Corrective Action ☐

    b)   Reviewing Stage Status ☐

    c)   Escalating Project Issues ☐

    d)   Reporting Highlights ☐

75.   Which is the missing section of the suggested Project File, if the others are Organisation, Plans, Business Case, Communication Plan and Control?

    a)   Correspondence ☐

    b)   Daily Log ☐

    c)   Risk Log ☐

    d)   Issue Log ☐

    e)   PID ☐

Total Score:

Marking your paper

Now you have completed the sample Foundation Examination paper, check your answers against those shown in the following table and look up the page number references in the manual for any questions you answered incorrectly. Page numbers are from the 2005 edition. You should, ideally, be looking for a score of between 60 and 65 correct answers and completion within 40 to 50 minutes. Remember, for the actual examination you need to score 38 correct answers in 60 minutes.

Table 1 Answer sheet

Q	Answer	Page		Q	Answer	Page		Q	Answer	Page
1	B	6		26	D	225		51	D	246
2	D	315		27	B	266		52	D	108
3	C	54		28	B	329		53	C	282
4	D	7		29	D	108		54	A	103
5	B	37/38		30	C	15		55	A	133
6	D	120		31	B	317		56	B	205
7	C	153		32	B	246		57	B	69
8	C	331		33	C	7		58	C	137
9	D	98		34	C	253		59	B	26
10	D	339		35	A	163		60	B	421
11	C	282		36	C	315		61	A	321
12	D	13		37	A	302/3		62	C	246
13	D	297		38	D	272/326		63	C	253
14	B	325		39	D	201		64	D	266
15	D	7		40	C	206		65	B	275
16	B	203		41	B	223		66	C	130
17	D	276		42	A	26		67	D	15
18	D	158		43	C	300		68	D	171
19	D	3		44	B	225		69	C	87
20	B	256		45	A	247		70	B	138
21	C	195		46	A	53		71	D	27
22	D	174		47	B	315		72	A	51
23	A	275		48	D	282		73	B	136
24	B	8		49	C	96		74	C	121
25	B	286		50	A	50		75	C	421

The Practitioner Examination

Introduction

The objectives of the examination are to enable a candidate to demonstrate to the examiner an understanding of PRINCE2 and an ability to apply the methodology in an appropriate way in a given set of circumstances described in a scenario. The Practitioner Examination uses objective testing questions which require a student to choose a response to a question from a set of choices for which the correct answer is predetermined.

The following paragraphs explain the format of the question papers, and the different types of question asked. There are also some suggestions on how to approach answering the various types of question.

Structure of the paper

The examination paper consists of three booklets.

The *Scenario Booklet* will contain one scenario providing a description of the organisation, the business rationale for the project and the project objectives. The *Scenario Booklet* may also provide additional information for one or more of the nine questions. Where this additional information is required it will be clearly referenced within the relevant question and should only be used for that question.

The combination of the scenario, each question and any additional information referenced in the *Scenario Booklet* will always 'position' both the candidate (to consider a particular PRINCE2 role) and the project (in terms of the timescale, e.g. in the middle of a stage or at the end of a project). The role to be considered will be at a level suitable for a delegate who has recently attended the PRINCE2 Practitioner course.

The *Question Booklet* will contain nine questions, each covering a different syllabus topic, which will be clearly identified within the question. Each of the nine questions is worth 40 marks. This gives a total of 360 marks. The pass mark is 180. Each of the nine questions will be sub-divided into parts. Each of the 'part-questions' will identify the portion of the 40 marks allocated to it. All questions and part-questions are expected to be answered.

The *Answer Booklet* will contain the answer sheets on which your answers must be given. There will only ever be one answer to each question unless it is otherwise clearly stated within the question. For some questions, negative marks will be applied for incorrect answers. This is clearly stated within each question to which this applies.

PRINCE2 topics addressed

The examination will consist of nine questions which will cover nine out of the 11 areas of the PRINCE2 Practitioner syllabus. The 'overview and principles' syllabus area will not be examined separately but details from this syllabus section may be included in the questions on each of the other syllabus areas.

Types of question

There are a number of different question types used within the paper.

These are:

- **Classic multiple choice questions** – choose one from a list of possible answers

- **Yes/No** – assess whether a statement is correct. 'Yes' or 'No' (chosen as the standard for 'True/False' type questions)

- **Multiple response** – choose the correct options from a list, remembering to limit the number of responses to that requested in each question. If more responses are given than required by the question, the answer will be void

- **Matching** – link items in one list to items in a second list. There is only one correct response to each question, but options can usually be used more than once or not at all

- **Sequencing** – position events in a sequence

- **Assertion/reason** – each item consists of two statements, an assertion and a reason that are linked by the word 'because'. First the candidate must determine whether the 'assertion' is true or false and then whether the 'reason' is true or false. If both are true, a third step is required and the candidate must determine whether the reason is a correct explanation for the assertion.

Question difficulty

Part-questions will vary in their level of difficulty depending on the learning objective of the test. The difficulty levels are:

- Knowledge
- Comprehension
- Application
- Analysis
- Evaluation

Within a question, the part-questions will be assembled in order of ascending difficulty level, with more marks being allocated to the responses for the more difficult questions.

The focus of the examination is on application, analysis and evaluation learning objectives. For each question, only 12 marks or less (of the total 40 marks) will be awarded for knowledge and comprehension part-questions.

For knowledge and comprehension questions marks to the value of the correct answer will also be subtracted for incorrect answers.

A summary description of each difficulty level and example syllabus topics it tests is given below.

Knowledge

This tests **knowledge of terminology and key principles** within PRINCE2 and examines recall of manual detail. This competency maps to syllabus statement 'know'.

Examples of topics tested include:

- identifying from a list, the statements that correctly describe the purpose of a product or the objectives of a process

- identifying the products involved in the controlled start of a project

- identifying Project Manager or Project Board controls.

Comprehension

This is the demonstration of **understanding of PRINCE2 concepts**. Typically this tests the grasping of meaning and the interpretation of wording that is different from the standard paragraphs in the PRINCE2 manual. This competency maps to the syllabus statement 'understand'.

Examples of topics tested include:

- assessing whether statements are a benefit of a product/technique/component

- identifying which products are updated in a project process or used as inputs to creating/updating a product

- matching generic descriptions of PRINCE2 activities to roles

- identifying correct descriptions of a product's content/process activities.

Application

Application refers to the ability to **apply PRINCE2 components, techniques and products** to a given project situation. This competency maps to the syllabus statements 'apply' (referring to a component or technique) and 'produce'.

In the objective test format candidates cannot actually create products, but this competency can still be tested, for example by using 'matching questions' that require candidates to match statements to the correct product composition heading.

Other possibilities include testing Product Breakdown Structure or Product Flow Diagram creation by using partially blank diagrams for which candidates have to identify correct products from a list to match the blank product.

Examples of test topics include:

- identifying how a product is impacted/updated in a given project situation

- matching candidates in a scenario to organisation roles

- identifying suitable customer's quality expectations/Acceptance Criteria for a given scenario

- matching risk responses to risk action types for a given project

- identifying the impact on a product of a given scenario situation.

Analysis

This is the competency to **analyse the use of the method**. This is NOT the ability to use analysis techniques such as risk analysis and product-based planning – **these are tested as an application competency**.

Typically this would test the ability to identify errors in the application of PRINCE2 or to identify the aspects of a PRINCE2 component or technique that could be of benefit in a given project situation.

To answer these kinds of questions candidates must have breadth of understanding of the topic, understand how that component/process/technique interacts with other components/processes/techniques and the implications of this for a given project scenario.

Examples of test topics include:

- identifying specific control problems on a project and the changes in control products that will address the problems

- assessing errors in a PRINCE2 management product, e.g. Quality Plan, Business Case

- identifying the errors in a Product Breakdown Structure or a Product Flow Diagram

- identifying specific Configuration Management problems in a project scenario situation.

Evaluation

This is the ability to **evaluate or justify the use of the method** in a given project situation. It is closely linked to the analysis competency but builds on this by requiring the candidate to explain or justify the recommendations they have made. It maps to the syllabus statements 'modify or discuss', 'discuss the application of' and 'justify the use of'.

Examples of test topics include:

- identifying reasons for unsatisfactory aspects in project controls

- identifying reasons for inadequacies in a PRINCE2 product, e.g. Quality Log, Project Quality Plan

- matching explanations to proposals for project controls/staging

- identifying reasons for a proposed project organisation or changes to it.

Sample PRINCE2 Practitioner Objective Test Scenario Booklet

The Practitioner Examination

This is a three-hour objective test, effective from 1 September 2007. This booklet contains the Project Scenario upon which all the questions are based. All questions are contained within the *Question Booklet*.

Additional information is provided within this booklet for a number of questions. Where additional information should be referenced, this is clearly stated within the question to which it is relevant. All information provided within a question must only be applied to that question.

Each of the nine questions is worth 40 marks, giving a maximum of 360 marks in the paper. You need to achieve a score of 50% averaged over the nine questions to pass this paper. Within each question the syllabus area to which the question refers is clearly stated.

In some questions incorrect choices will result in marks being deducted. This is clearly stated in the question. Answers left blank will score zero. The examination is to be taken with the support of the PRINCE2 Manual only, i.e. no material other than the *Question Booklet*, the *Scenario Booklet*, the *Answer Booklet* and the PRINCE2 Manual can be used. Please read and follow the instructions below carefully.

Instructions

1   You should attempt to answer all nine questions.

2   Answers should be indicated by marking the corresponding area on the *Answer Booklet* in pencil.

3   Do not use coloured pens or highlighters on the *Answer Booklet*.

4   Do not use white fluid.

5   If you wish to change an answer, simply erase your original marks and place a mark in your preferred answer.

6   All questions have one answer unless specifically stated in the question. If more than the required number of answers is given, the question will score zero.

Candidate Number: ....

Project scenario

The MNO Manufacturing Company is experiencing a fall in orders due in part to the increased marketing operations of its competitors. To help counter this, it has been decided to create a Calendar for next year for all its customers and prospective customers. You have been chosen as the Project Manager.

The end product of the project will be a Prepared Calendar Pack ready for printing. This will consist of:

- 12 Monthly Calendar Displays reflecting the layout of each page

- a set of 12 Photos selected for inclusion in the Calendar

- the Selected Paper and Envelope

- a Label Design for the Envelope chosen from a Competition to be held as part of the project

- a List of Customers to whom the Calendar will be sent compiled from information supplied by the Accounts and Marketing Departments.

The Calendar Pack should be ready for printing and delivered to the printers by 30 November; however, there is a time tolerance of +2 weeks/-1 week.

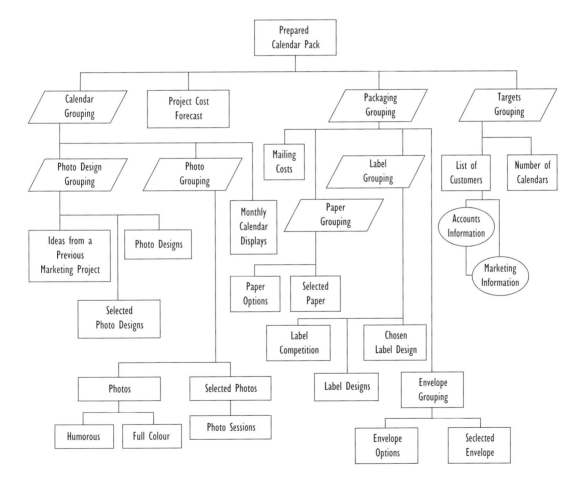

Product Breakdown Structure (with technical and content errors)

Possible project resources

This is a list of company personnel plus external resources that may have a part to play in the project.

Managing Director: This is the person who had the idea of the Calendar. He started the company 25 years ago. He injured his leg two years ago; this has restricted his visits to the engineering area.

Marketing Director: Has been with the company three years. She had a successful career with a publicity company but has taken some time to adjust to selling to the engineering industry.

Engineering Manager: Has been with the company 25 years, starting as an apprentice and working his way through the ranks. He has been responsible for many engineering innovations in the company and is still as keen and energetic as the day he started.

Finance Manager: Has been with the company 17 years and knows her job very well.

Personnel Manager: Knows the staff well and keeps a close eye on the local and national employment situation as well as the engineering wages.

Purchasing Manager: Leads a team of three. They set up all the contracts for the company, both with suppliers and customers. He is an engineer and worked in that area for 10 years before taking up his current position.

Sales Manager: Joined the company last year with huge enthusiasm and is convinced that with the Calendar his team can improve the sales position.

Central Records: This group of five staff looks after all engineering records. The section was created many years ago after the company lost the drawing records for a complex product.

Central Records Manager: He is a keen photographer. He has offered to take the Photos for the price of the film.

Administration: This group of four looks after all secretarial work, any travel arrangements, hotel and conference arrangements.

Bright Lights: This is the local office supplies company. It supplies all the stationery and office equipment needs of the company and will supply the stationery for this project.

Post office manager: He is nearing retirement after a lifetime's work for the Post Office.

Portraits Ltd: This is the local professional photographer with a long background of successful work. He is expensive, but offers a long track record of successful pictures and has been chosen to take the Photos for the company Calendar.

Sample PRINCE2 Practitioner Question Booklet

The Practitioner Examination

Candidate Number: ....

Syllabus areas covered

Question 1 – Plans

Question 2 – Management of Risk

Question 3 – Controls

Question 4 – Product-based planning

Question 5 – Configuration Management

Question 6 – Change Control

Question 7 – Processes

Question 8 – Business Case

Question 9 – Quality in a project environment

Question number: 1

Syllabus area: Plans

At the end of stage 2 the chosen photographer was appointed as Team Manager, and the Paper and Envelopes were chosen for the Calendar.

Stage 3 is about to begin, during which the Photos of engineering staff will be taken and selected, the Label Design Competition will be held and the winning Label Design chosen. Although the Stage Plan has tolerances on time and cost, no tolerances have been allocated to the photographer's Work Package for extra photo shoots.

Syllabus Area	Question Number	Part	Marks
Plans	1	A	2

Each type of PRINCE2 plan has its own purpose, objectives and content.

Column 1 contains statements about the PRINCE2 plans. Column 2 lists four of the PRINCE2 types of plan. Review each of the statements in Column 1 and select the plan from Column 2 that **most** applies to the information in the statement. A selection from Column 2 may be used more than once or not at all. Marks will be subtracted for incorrect answers in this question.

	Column 1		Column 2
1	The need for this plan is determined by the size and complexity of the project.	A	Project Plan
2	The basis for the Project Board to monitor actual costs and project progress stage by stage.	B	Stage Plan
3	Identifies key products, resource requirements and the total costs.	C	Team Plan
4	Prepared at the same time as the Stage Plan.	D	Exception Plan

Syllabus Area	Question Number	Part	Marks
Plans	1	B	20

When the Project Manager prepared the Stage Plan for stage 3 of the project, there was a lot of information to consider for inclusion.

Review the information in Column 1 and select the plan heading from Column 2 in which it is **most likely** to be recorded. A selection from Column 2 may be used more than once or not at all.

	Column 1		Column 2
1	Project Assurance has been assigned to review progress during stage 3.	A	Plan description
2	The Project Manager requires regular progress information from the photographer.	B	Stage quality plan
3	The Project Manager believes that the availability of engineering staff for the Photo Sessions may be minimal due to their current workload and he must allow for delays.	C	Plan prerequisites
4	The company's Marketing Department will take responsibility for checking the work carried out by the professional photographer.	D	External dependencies
5	The Project Manager is aware of potential forthcoming changes to the List of Customers who will be receiving the Calendar.	E	How the plan will be monitored and controlled
6	Customer details, and any changes to these, will be supplied from the Sales and Marketing departmental customer databases. These databases are being maintained within the individual departments.	F	Reporting
7	The Marketing forecast must indicate at least a 15% increase in orders each year for the next three years if the photography and Label Competition are to go ahead.	G	Planning assumptions
8	Each Photo must contain at least one member of staff.	H	Risk assessment

9	For the Label Competition to be successful, the staff must be encouraged to take part.	I	Product Descriptions
10	The Engineering Manager was unavailable when the Project Manager was preparing the Schedule for the Photo Sessions therefore the Project Manager used previous staff schedules as a basis for the photo schedule.		

Syllabus Area	Question Number	Part	Marks
Plans	1	C	18

Lines 1 to 6 in the table below consist of an assertion statement and a reason statement. For each line identify the appropriate selection from options A to E that applies. A selection may be used more than once or not at all.

Selection	Assertion	Reason	
A	True	True	Reason is a correct explanation of the assertion
B	True	True	Reason is correct but not an explanation for the assertion
C	True	False	
D	False	True	
E	False	False	

	Assertion		Reason
1	A Team Plan will be produced by the Project Manager at the beginning of stage 3 for the production of the Photos.	BECAUSE	The photographer should have a Team Plan for the creation of the Photos because specialist knowledge is required.
2	If an additional Photo Session is required for the photographs, the Project Manager should create an Exception Plan.	BECAUSE	The photographer should update the Stage Plan to reflect the additional resources required for another Photo Session.
3	The Engineering Manager should produce the stage 3 plan.	BECAUSE	The stage 3 plan includes the Schedule for the Photo Sessions, which impacts engineering staff.
4	The Project Plan should provide input into the planning of stage 3.	BECAUSE	The Project Plan should be updated with details of the time and cost estimates for the products being delivered in stage 3.
5	The Quality Review of the Photos should be planned as part of the stage 3 plan.	BECAUSE	The stage 3 plan should incorporate all activities to ensure that the products in stage 3 meet their stated quality criteria.
6	Detailed activities for each stage should always be added to the Project Plan.	BECAUSE	The Project Plan must show the day-to-day activities of all those working on the project.

Question number: 2

Syllabus area: Management of Risk

Syllabus Area	Question Number	Part	Marks
Management of Risk	2	A	16

Having reviewed the costs, the Managing Director has agreed to proceed with the Calendar project.

The project is in progress when the Project Manager hears about the possibility of a major rival also producing a Calendar to be delivered earlier than the target date for this project. There is a risk that the early release of a rival Calendar will reduce the benefits anticipated. Following a risk analysis the Project Manager has identified the risk responses listed in Column 1. Match these responses to the appropriate action type in Column 2. A selection from Column 2 may be used more than once or not at all.

	Column 1		Column 2
1	Get the Central Records Manager, the keen photographer, to take some initial Photos so that the quality of his work can be assessed and compared to that of a professional. He could be used to bring the target date for the project forward.	A	Prevention
2	Cancel the project, deciding not to compete.	B	Reduction
3	Bring the target date of this project forward to beat the competitor.	C	Transference
4	Wait for confirmation of the rival's Calendar and, if required, include additional gifts with the Calendar as an extra incentive.	D	Acceptance
5	Get a copy of the rival's Calendar so that the Project Manager can ensure the quality of the MNO Calendar is better or it contains more.	E	Contingency
6	Carry on with the project as planned on the basis that the Project Manager believes the MNO Calendar will be of better quality.		
7	Provide advance notice to customers about the planned launch of the Calendar.		
8	In order to ensure the Calendar is of the best quality and delivered earlier than the competitors, outsource the creation of the Calendar to a professional marketing company.		

Syllabus Area	Question Number	Part	Marks
Management of Risk	2	B	24

A photographer from Portraits Ltd, a professional photographic company, has taken on the role of Team Manager after taking some time to understand the requirements of the project. He should have arranged a meeting with the Engineering Manager to establish a Photo Session Schedule designed to minimise the impact on the Engineering staff.

Reports back from the Engineering Manager are that there has been no contact with this photographer. The Project Manager has tried to call him and has had no response. The Project Manager believes there is a risk that the company is overbooking work and prioritising other clients' work, which may put the project deadline at risk.

Lines 1 to 5 in the table below consist of an assertion statement and a reason statement. For each line identify the appropriate selection from options A to E that applies. A selection may be used more than once or not at all.

Selection	Assertion	Reason	
A	True	True	Reason is a correct explanation of the assertion
B	True	True	Reason is correct but not an explanation for the assertion
C	True	False	
D	False	True	
E	False	False	

	Assertion		Reason
1	The Engineering Manager should have raised this concern as a Project Issue.	BECAUSE	Any delay in producing the Photo Session Schedule could have an impact on the project timescales.
2	The lack of contact with the photographer should have been raised as a Project Issue as it leads to a new risk.	BECAUSE	A risk can become a Project Issue and a Project Issue can identify a new risk.
3	The risk should be categorised as organisational/management.	BECAUSE	All risks should be categorised to assist in their identification and evaluation.
4	The risk that the photographer may be prioritising other clients' work should be owned by the Purchasing Manager, who is responsible for setting up and monitoring supplier contracts.	BECAUSE	The risk owner is the person responsible for managing the risk and taking corrective action.
5	The photographer should have raised any concerns about their availability for the work as a risk when they accepted the Work Package.	BECAUSE	A separate Risk Log should be created for each Work Package to monitor specialist risks associated with the creation of specialist products.

A photographer from Portraits Ltd, a professional photographic company, has taken on the role of Team Manager after taking some time to understand the requirements of the project. He should have arranged a meeting with the Engineering Manager to establish a Photo Session Schedule designed to minimise the impact on the Engineering staff.

Reports back from the Engineering Manager are that there has been no contact with this photographer. The Project Manager has tried to call him and has had no response. The Project Manager believes there is a risk that the company is overbooking work and prioritising other clients' work, which may put the project deadline at risk.

Lines 6 to 8 in the table below consist of an assertion statement and a reason statement. For each line identify the appropriate selection from options A to E that applies. A selection may be used more than once or not at all.

Selection	Assertion	Reason	
A	True	True	Reason is a correct explanation of the assertion
B	True	True	Reason is correct but not an explanation for the assertion
C	True	False	
D	False	True	
E	False	False	

	Assertion		Reason
6	If evaluation of the risk shows that it is likely to impact on time, the Project Manager will need to raise a Project Issue.	BECAUSE	Any risk that is evaluated to have a high impact on time, cost, quality, scope, benefits or people/resources should be raised as a Project Issue.
7	In order to monitor the risk, the Project Manager should insist on regular Checkpoint Reports from the photographer throughout the duration of the Work Package.	BECAUSE	Regular Checkpoint Reports should ensure that the Project Manager is regularly updated on the status of the work and will get early warning of any delay in the photographer's work.
8	As a Work Package has been agreed with the photographer, the Project Manager should accept this risk and assume that the photographer has everything under control.	BECAUSE	When selecting the most appropriate risk action to take, the best option is usually the cheapest.

Question number: 3

Syllabus area: Controls

Syllabus Area	Question Number	Part	Marks
Controls	3	A	6

As part of the project, the Project Manager will deal with three suppliers:

● A local office stationer who will provide a number of Paper and Envelope options, then later provide in volume the Selected Paper and Envelopes

● The local post office manager who will provide Mailing Costs according to the weight and size of the Calendar for a number of Paper and Envelope Options

● A photographer to take the Photos. The photographer will be provided with Photo Designs and asked for a date for taking the Photos to allow the Schedule to be produced of who is needed on the Photos and the times. The photographer may bring an assistant to help with setting up each Photo and placing the lighting.

For each of the suppliers answer the following questions. **You may select more than one answer where appropriate.** Marks will be subtracted for incorrect answers in this question.

1	To which of the suppliers would the Project Manager allocate a Team Manager role?	
	A	Local office stationer
	B	Local post office manager
	C	Photographer
2	From which of the suppliers would the Project Manager request a Checkpoint Report?	
	A	Local office stationer
	B	Local post office manager
	C	Photographer
3	Which of the suppliers can raise a Project Issue?	
	A	Local office stationer
	B	Local post office manager
	C	Photographer
4	Which of the suppliers would be expected to update the Quality Log?	
	A	Local office stationer
	B	Local post office manager
	C	Photographer

Syllabus Area	Question Number	Part	Marks
Controls	3	B	16

A review of progress against the final Stage Plan, and its subsequent impact on the Project Plan, shows that the delivery date will be three weeks beyond the 30 November target date. The stage has no cost or time tolerances remaining. The project has no time tolerance remaining and a cost tolerance of £+10,000. Indicate the sequence of the first three actions that the Project Manager would take. For the remaining options indicate if they would be relevant subsequent actions or not relevant actions.

	Column 1		Column 2
1	Raise an Exception Report.	A	First choice
2	Raise a risk.	B	Second choice
3	Carry on and enter 'high' against risk tolerance.	C	Third choice
4	Stop work until decision made by Project Board.	D	Relevant
5	Consider the options available to deal with the delay.	E	Not relevant
6	Ask for the remaining cost tolerance to secure resources to recover the three weeks.		
7	Raise a Project Issue.		
8	Recommend that the project continues and the Business Case is revised to reduce benefits because of late delivery.		

Syllabus Area	Question Number	Part	Marks
Controls	3	C	18

Lines 1 to 6 in the table below consist of an assertion statement and a reason statement. For each line identify the appropriate selection from options A to E that applies. A selection may be used more than once or not at all.

Selection	Assertion	Reason	
A	True	True	Reason is a correct explanation of the assertion
B	True	True	Reason is correct but not an explanation for the assertion
C	True	False	
D	False	True	
E	False	False	

	Assertion		Reason
1	The Label Competition should be managed in two stages.	BECAUSE	The selection of the final Label Design indicates a decision point for the Project Board and this can only be done at a stage break.
2	Quality tolerances allocated to the Photos can be used to remedy a forecast threat to time tolerance.	BECAUSE	The setting of a tolerance type may have an impact on the setting of another tolerance type.
3	A suitable point for a stage break should be after the Managing Director and Marketing Director have reviewed the Forecast Project Cost based on the Mailing, Paper and Envelope costs.	BECAUSE	The Forecast Project Cost will be a key input to the decision point on whether or not to continue with the project.

4	The Photo Sessions should form a separate stage.	BECAUSE	The Photo Sessions should be managed as part of the Work Package agreed with the chosen photographer.
5	The time tolerance quoted in the scenario means that the project can finish two weeks earlier or one week later than 30 November.	BECAUSE	The time tolerance quoted in the scenario means that every management stage can finish up to two weeks later than the planned end date.
6	The photographer should be given a tolerance for both cost and time in order to ensure the required quality of Photos is achieved.	BECAUSE	When agreeing work with suppliers, tolerance can be given to allow for any minor changes to the agreed schedule.

Question number: 4

Syllabus area: Product-based planning

The Managing Director said he was hoping for a Calendar on top-quality glossy paper in full colour. To create this Calendar, a List of Customers will need to be assembled. This will use information from the Accounts Department about current customers, and information from the Marketing Department about prospective customers. The Project Manager must also provide options for the Paper on which the calendars are to be printed and, based on the weight of the various Paper Options, options on the Envelopes in which to post the Calendar. These options will have to be gathered from a local office supplies company. Discussions will then be required with the Post Office about the Mailing Costs based on the Number of Calendars and the various Envelopes.

Based on the Mailing Costs, the Paper Options and the Envelope Options, a Forecast of the Project Cost is needed to allow the Managing Director and the Marketing Director to decide whether to continue with the project. If they decide to continue, they will at that point select the Paper and Envelope, give the signal to do the Photo Designs and launch an Internal Label Competition.

The Photo Designs for the Calendar must be based on Ideas from a Previous Marketing Project.

After the Marketing Director has chosen the Photo Designs, Photo Sessions will be required to create a number of Photos. The Engineering Manager is keen to minimise interruptions to work due to his staff being photographed, so a Schedule is required for the Photo Sessions. The Schedule will not be created until the Managing Director and Marketing Director have agreed to continue with the project.

A Design is required for the Label to be put on the Envelope. As part of the project, an Internal Competition will be held for Designs for this Label, from which the final choice will be made. The standard Company Logo needs to be integrated into the Label Design.

The Prepared Calendar Pack will then be assembled from the Monthly Calendar Displays, the Selected Photos, the Chosen Paper and Envelope, the Chosen Label Design and the List of Customers.

Syllabus Area	Question Number	Part	Marks
Product-based planning	4	A	10

Using the scenario and the Product Breakdown Structure (PBS) in the *Scenario Booklet*, answer the following five questions. There is only one correct answer to each question.

1		'Ideas from Previous Marketing Project' should be:
	A	external product
	B	source
	C	internal product developed by an external supplier
	D	removed as it is not a product
2		'Full Colour' is shown in the diagram. Which of the following best describe this?
	A	description that properly belongs in the *Derivation* section of the Product Description
	B	description that properly belongs in the *Format and Presentation* section of the Product Description
	C	description that properly belongs in the *Quality Criteria* section of the Product Description
	D	description that properly belongs in the *Composition* section of the Product Description
3		The 'Company Logo' needs to be added to the plan. How should the 'Company Logo' be represented in the PBS?
	A	ellipse
	B	rectangle
	C	rhomboid
	D	it shouldn't because it is not part of the project
4		Which of the following products should have been included in the PBS?
	A	Engineering Staff
	B	Glossy Paper
	C	Photographer
	D	Session Schedule
5		As the PBS is drawn, what type of product is the 'List of Customers' product?
	A	simple product
	B	external product
	C	integration product
	D	collective grouping

Syllabus Area	Question Number	Part	Marks
Product-based planning	4	B	30

Column 1 is a list of some of the specialist products from the Product Breakdown Structure (PBS) diagram in the *Scenario Booklet*. Determine whether each product in Column 1 has been correctly shown in the PBS by selecting the appropriate statement from Column 2 that correctly describes that product. A selection from Column 2 may be used more than once or not at all.

	Column 1		Column 2
1	Project Cost Forecast	A	Incorrectly joined to another product
2	Mailing Costs	B	Product does not consist of its sub-product(s)
3	Ideas from Previous Marketing Project	C	Incorrectly shown in a one-to-one relationship
4	Photo Designs	D	Intermediate product not shown correctly

5	Accounts Information	E	Integration product not shown correctly
6	Monthly Calendar Displays	F	External product not shown correctly
7	Photo Sessions	G	Simple product incorrectly shown as an external product
8	Selected Photos	H	Not a product
9	Envelope Grouping	I	Correctly shown product
10	Photo Design Grouping		

Question number: 5

Syllabus area: Configuration Management

Syllabus Area	Question Number	Part	Marks
Configuration Management	5	A	2

Which one of the following represents the most sensible configuration identification scheme for the 'January Photo' from this project.

		Identification Scheme
1	A	Cal/Engineering/Photo/January/V1.0
	B	Cal/Specialist/Photo/V1.0/Engineering
	C	Cal/Photo/January/V1.0
	D	Cal/Photo/V1.0/GB
	E	Cal/Photo/Specialist/January/V1.0

Syllabus Area	Question Number	Part	Marks
Configuration Management	5	B	14

The information in Column 1 about the Photos for the Calendar project needs to be entered into a Configuration Item Record. Identify under which of the headings of the Configuration Item Record in Column 2 each item of information should be recorded. A selection from Column 2 may be used more than once or not at all.

	Column 1		Column 2
1	Issued for review.	A	Lifecycle steps appropriate to the product
2	Project Issue 95 asked for darker colours to be used.	B	Owner of the product
3	Photos would be used as part of the Monthly Calendar Displays.	C	Person working on the product
4	The photographer who will be providing the Photos.	D	Source
5	The photographer's contract outlines the requirement for the Photos.	E	Links to related products
6	The printer will need a copy of the Photos.	F	Status

| 7 | Photos will be maintained by the Marketing Department. | G | Copy holders and potential users |
| | | H | Cross-reference to the Project Issue(s) that caused the change |

Syllabus Area	Question Number	Part	Marks
Configuration Management	5	C	24

There is a major concern over an apparent lack of control of project documentation. For each concern listed in Column 1 below, select the action from Column 2 which would have **best** addressed the problem. A selection from Column 2 may be used more than once or not at all.

	Column 1		Column 2
1	As a number of people are involved in the project it is becoming increasingly difficult to keep track of who has what.	A	Create an identification scheme
2	Both current and previous versions of the Photo Schedule are in circulation.	B	Configuration Librarian maintains current product status
3	No one can tell which of the Photo Schedules in circulation is the latest version.	C	Configuration Librarian to record who has copies
4	Marketing needed a copy of the chosen Label Design, but couldn't find it.	D	Link between version and the Project Issue that caused its change
5	Marketing staff could not say with any certainty which Photos were approved and which still required work.	E	Notify copy holders of any changes
6	The Engineering Manager complained that marketing staff had changed the Photo Schedule but that no advice about the change had been given to the engineering department.	F	Recall superseded versions
7	Marketing will use a number of the Photos for this year's company Christmas cards.	G	Configuration Librarian to hold master copies
8	No one has considered what impact changes to the Photo Schedule will have on the photographer's contract.	H	Maintain a record of relationships between products

Question number: 6

Syllabus area: Change Control

It is the end of October, and the project is part way through stage 3. There is no time tolerance left and only £+10,000 cost tolerance remaining for the project.

The Customer List, derived from the Accounts Department's List of Current Customers and the Marketing Department's List of Prospective Customers, has been compiled, reviewed and signed off. The Label Design Competition has been held, but the winning Label Design has yet to be chosen. The Paper and Envelopes for the Calendar have been chosen.

Syllabus Area	Question Number	Part	Marks
Change Control	6	A	5

	There have been rumours of a competitor launching a similar marketing product to our customers before us. These rumours have now been confirmed and will have a major impact on the success of the Calendar.
1	Raise an Exception Report for the Project Board presenting the options available to them.
2	Evaluate the Project Issue in terms of its impact on the stage and project tolerances.
3	Hold an Exception Assessment.
4	Raise a Project Issue and log it in the Issue Log.
5	Produce an Exception Plan.
1	Which of the following sequences correctly represents the order in which the Project Manager should carry out the above activities?

	A	4, 2, 1, 5, 3
	B	4, 2, 1, 3, 5
	C	2, 4, 1, 5, 3
	D	2, 4, 1, 3, 5
	E	4, 1, 2, 5, 3

Syllabus Area	Question Number	Part	Marks
Change Control	6	B	5

The Project Board agreed to bring the launch date of the Calendar forward by using the internal photographer to produce the Photos. Which of the following PRINCE2 management products should the Project Manager **update** in preparation for the Exception Assessment? For each of the statements in Column 1 select either A (Yes, this product is updated) or B (No, this product is NOT updated). Marks will be subtracted for incorrect answers in this question.

	Column 1		Column 2
1	Business Case	A	Yes, this product is updated
2	Highlight Report	B	No, this product is NOT updated
3	End Stage Report		
4	Project Plan		
5	Risk Log		
6	Checkpoint Report		
7	Photographer's Work Package		
8	Communication Plan		
9	Lessons Learned Log		
10	Project Approach		

Syllabus Area	Question Number	Part	Marks
Change Control	6	C	12

Consider each of the statements in Column 1. Select from Column 2 the option which best describes each statement. A selection from Column 2 may be used more than once or not at all.

	Column 1		Column 2
1	Although not previously considered, the Engineering Manager now wants to include his latest production machinery in some of the Photos.	A	Request for Change
2	The Marketing Director is concerned that the Calendar will not be of sufficient quality to achieve the projected benefits.	B	Off-Specification
3	Marketing has identified some prospective customers and wants to include them in the Approved Customer List.	C	New risk
4	Following the Quality Review and sign off of the Monthly Calendar Displays a member of the project team asked for statutory holidays to be identified as stated in the Product Description.	D	Project Issue
5	Following the Quality Review and sign off of the Chosen Label Design, it is discovered that an old version of the Company Logo has been used.		
6	There has been a rumour of a postal strike occurring in December. The Project Manager has now received confirmation that this will happen.		

Syllabus Area	Question Number	Part	Marks
Change Control	6	D	18

Lines 1 to 6 in the table below consist of an assertion statement and a reason statement. For each line identify the appropriate selection from options A to E that applies. A selection may be used more than once or not at all.

Selection	Assertion	Reason	
A	True	True	Reason is a correct explanation of the assertion
B	True	True	Reason is correct but not an explanation for the assertion
C	True	False	
D	False	True	
E	False	False	
	Assertion	Reason	
1	Any forecast delay to the project will now require an Exception Report.	BECAUSE	If a delay is forecast, the Project Manager could recommend the use of cost tolerance to reduce the delay.

2	As a Team Manager, the Photographer should be given a copy of the Project Quality Plan in order to understand the Change Control process which he must work within.	BECAUSE	The Change Control Approach is defined in the Project Quality Plan.
3	If marketing identifies new customers to be added to the Approved Customer List, a Request for Change is NOT required.	BECAUSE	The source Customer Lists from Accounts and Marketing are external to this project and we have no authority to change them.
4	The Marketing Director has requested that each customer receive a company-branded pen with their Calendar, at a total cost of £2,000. The Project Manager does NOT need to obtain authorisation from the Project Board for this change.	BECAUSE	The remaining cost tolerance can be allocated by the Project Manager to pay for the issue of company-branded pens with the Calendar.
5	The Selected Paper, once approved by the Marketing Director and Managing Director, can only be changed by the submission of a Project Issue.	BECAUSE	As an approved product, the Selected Paper is baselined in the Configuration Management System.
6	If a suitable Label Design is NOT found, there is sufficient cost tolerance within the project to cover the estimated £2,000 to get a design produced professionally.	BECAUSE	Cost tolerance can be used to change how a product is delivered as long as the final product is unchanged.

Question number: 7

Syllabus area: Processes

Syllabus Area	Question Number	Part	Marks
Processes	7	A	3

Consider each objective in Column 1 and decide which are objectives of the initiation stage. From options in Column 2 select either A (Yes, this is an objective of the initiation stage) or B (No, this is NOT an objective of the initiation stage). Marks will be subtracted for incorrect answers in this question.

	Column 1		Column 2
1	It documents and confirms that an acceptable Business Case exists for this project.	A	Yes, this is an objective of the initiation stage.
2	It approves the appointment of the Project Manager and the Executive for this project.	B	No, this is NOT an objective of the initiation stage.
3	It enables and encourages the Project Board to take ownership of the project.		
4	It draws up 'a contract' between the Project Manager and the Project Board so that everyone has a common understanding of the project.		

| 5 | It helps define the Project Approach. | | |
| 6 | It helps define how the quality of the final product will be achieved. | | |

Syllabus Area	Question Number	Part	Marks
Processes	7	B	22

It is now late October and the project is in stage 3. A Competition has been held to create the Label Design for the Envelope in which the Calendar will be mailed, but the winning design has not yet been chosen. This Label Design will also be used for this year's company Christmas cards. The Photos have been taken and are of members of staff. To complete the stage, the Managing Director and Marketing Director need to choose the winning Label Design and 12 Photos to include in the Calendar. However, the Executive has learned that two competitors are issuing Calendars to our customers by the middle of November. After analysing the impact of this issue, one of the options the Project Manager has presented to the Project Board is to close the project prematurely.

There are a number of key facts relating to this project that would need to be recorded if the project were to be closed now.

Review each of the statements in Column 1 against the information given above and in the scenario and select the output from Column 2 **most likely** to use the information in the statement. A selection from Column 2 may be used more than once or not at all.

	Column 1		Column 2
1	The Photos could be used for other promotional material for the company.	A	Customer Acceptance
2	The Customer List has completed its quality check and has been signed off by the Senior User.	B	End Project Report
3	All resource costs should be charged to the project by 10 November.	C	Exception Report
4	The Managing Director and Marketing Director need to select the winning Label Design and announce the result.	D	Follow-on Actions Recommendations
5	Some increased sales can be generated by using the winning Label Design for this year's Christmas card.	E	Lessons Learned Report
6	The staff Photo Sessions were disruptive to the Engineering Department as they had been scheduled during peak work times without consultation with the Engineering Manager.	F	Operational and Maintenance Acceptance
7	Company staff must be notified of the decision to close the project.	G	Post-Project Review Plan
8	The project has been closed prematurely and has not achieved the objectives defined in the PID.	H	Project Closure Notification
		I	Risk Log

It is now late October and the project is in stage 3. A Competition has been held to create the Label Design for the Envelope in which the Calendar will be mailed, but the winning design has not yet been chosen. This Label Design will also be used for this year's company Christmas cards. The Photos have been taken and are of members of staff. To complete the stage, the Managing Director and Marketing Director need to choose the winning Label Design and 12 Photos to include in the Calendar. However, the Executive has learned that two competitors are issuing Calendars to our customers by the middle of November. After analysing the impact of this issue, one of the options the Project Manager has presented to the Project Board is to close the project prematurely.

There are a number of key facts relating to this project that would need to be recorded if the project were to be closed now.

Review each of the statements in Column 1 against the information given above and in the scenario and select the output from Column 2 **most likely** to use the information in the statement. A selection from Column 2 may be used more than once or not at all.

	Column 1		Column 2
9	Without the Calendar the company is going to experience difficulties recovering its fall in orders. Alternative solutions are required if the company is going to recover its position.	A	Customer Acceptance
10	There are damage clauses in the supplier contracts and cancellation of these contracts will need to be negotiated.	B	End Project Report
11	The risk of a competitor producing a Calendar at the same time was identified at the beginning of the project but the analysis of this risk appears to have been poor.	C	Exception Report
		D	Follow-on Actions Recommendations
		E	Lessons Learned Report
		F	Operational and Maintenance Acceptance
		G	Post-Project Review Plan
		H	Project Closure Notification
		I	Risk Log

Syllabus Area	Question Number	Part	Marks
Processes	7	C	15

Lines 1 to 5 in the table below consist of an assertion statement and a reason statement. For each line identify the appropriate selection from options A to E that applies. A selection may be used more than once or not at all.

Selection	Assertion	Reason	
A	True	True	Reason is a correct explanation of the assertion
B	True	True	Reason is correct but not an explanation for the assertion
C	True	False	
D	False	True	
E	False	False	

	Assertion	Reason	
1	The risk of not meeting the 30 November target date could not be accurately evaluated during the Starting Up a Project process.	BECAUSE	The Risk Log is created in the Initiating a Project process.
2	The detailed planning of the work to design the Envelope Label will be done during the Starting Up a Project process.	BECAUSE	The detailed planning of all Work Packages must be completed before commencement of the Initiating a Project process.
3	Whether the Calendar achieves its objective of countering the fall in orders will be finally checked in the Closing a Project process.	BECAUSE	The Post-Project Review Plan is created in the Closing a Project process.
4	The fact that the project is to try to counter the fall in orders would be documented in the Project Brief.	BECAUSE	The need to counter the fall in orders will form part of the outline Business Case.
5	The Managing Director and Marketing Director will decide whether they wish to continue with the project when the Mailing Costs are presented to them in an Exception Plan.	BECAUSE	The Mailing Costs are a one-off cost to the project and will need to be presented to the Project Board in an Exception Plan.

Question number: 8

Syllabus area: Business Case

Syllabus Area	Question Number	Part	Marks
Business Case	8	A	6

The activities in Column 1 are undertaken when developing and maintaining the Business Case throughout the PRINCE2 project lifecycle. Listed in Column 2 are six PRINCE2 roles.

For each of the activities in Column 1 select the role in Column 2 most likely to undertake them. A selection from Column 2 may be used more than once or not at all. Marks will be subtracted for incorrect answers in this question.

	Column 1		Column 2
1	Defining the benefits and ensuring they are aligned to an organisation's business strategy.	A	Executive
2	During Initiation, updating the Business Case with more detailed information on the risks, options and costs.	B	Project Manager
3	Recording the relationships between the documents of a complex Business Case for a large project.	C	Team Manager
4	Checking the revisions made to the Business Case before the stage end.	D	Configuration Librarian

| 5 | Formal approval of the Business Case. | E | Project Assurance |
| 6 | Developing the Business Case if delegated by the Executive. | F | Project Support |

Syllabus Area	Question Number	Part	Marks
Business Case	8	B	4

Column 1 is a list of true and false statements about when the Business Case is **updated**. For each of the statements in Column 1 select either A (Yes, this is correct) or B (No, this is incorrect). Marks will be subtracted for incorrect answers in this question.

	Column 1		Column 2
1	When raising an Exception Report.	A	Yes, this is correct
2	When preparing for an End Stage Assessment.	B	No, this is incorrect
3	When examining a Project Issue.		
4	When updating the Communication Plan.		
5	When analysing a risk.		
6	When preparing for an Exception Assessment.		
7	When updating a Configuration Item Record.		
8	When preparing the Post-Project Review Plan.		

Syllabus Area	Question Number	Part	Marks
Business Case	8	C	18

As the Business Case influences the decision-making processes on the project it must contain sufficient information to be used effectively throughout the project. Column 1 lists nine statements, some or all of which will be included in this project's Business Case. Determine for each statement in Column 1 whether it will be included and select from Column 2 under which heading it is **most likely** to be recorded. A selection from Column 2 may be used more than once or not at all.

	Column 1		Column 2
1	MNO is experiencing a fall in orders due in part to the increased marketing operations of its competitors.	A	Reasons
2	The Calendar Pack must be ready for printing by 30 November.	B	Options
3	A competitor may also be producing a Calendar for its customers.	C	Benefits
4	The Marketing Department forecast that issuing a Calendar to our customers will increase our orders for next year by 10%.	D	Risks
5	Staff availability for the Photo Session may cause delays to the completion date.	E	Costs
6	The Calendar will contain Photos of both staff and company products.	F	Timescales

7	The required outcome could be achieved by creating a Calendar for all our current customers and prospective customers.	G	Not applicable
8	The Marketing Department forecast that we could get a further 10 orders from new customers in year 2.		
9	The Executive will appoint the Finance Manager to perform the role of business assurance to monitor the Business Case.		

Syllabus Area	Question Number	Part	Marks
Business Case	8	D	12

Lines 1 to 4 in the table below consist of an assertion statement and a reason statement. For each line identify the appropriate selection from options A to E that applies. A selection may be used more than once or not at all.

Selection	Assertion	Reason	
A	True	True	Reason is a correct explanation of the assertion
B	True	True	Reason is correct but not an explanation for the assertion
C	True	False	
D	False	True	
E	False	False	

	Assertion	Reason	
1	The Business Case should be revised if Marketing's forecast for increased orders changes.	BECAUSE	The Business Case is an input to the Project Board in the decision to authorise a Stage or Exception Plan.
2	If the paper supplier changes there may be a review of, and possible changes to, the Business Case.	BECAUSE	The Business Case includes options for the delivery of the Calendar solution.
3	Provided the Calendars are available for printing before December, time tolerances will not be exceeded.	BECAUSE	The Business Case is deemed no longer viable if stage tolerances are exceeded during the project.
4	The fact that the project is to try to counter the fall in orders would be documented in the Project Brief.	BECAUSE	The outline Business Case is developed from the Project Mandate and forms part of the Project Brief.

Question number: 9

Syllabus area: Quality in a project environment

Syllabus Area	Question Number	Part	Marks
Quality in a project environment	9	A	4

Column 1 is a list of quality responsibilities within a PRINCE2 project. For each responsibility in Column 1 select the role from Column 2 that should perform it. A selection from Column 2 may be used more than once or not at all. Marks will be subtracted for incorrect answers in this question.

	Column 1		Column 2
1	Ensuring the right people are involved in writing quality criteria for Product Descriptions.	A	Executive
2	Agreeing the supplier standards to be met.	B	Senior User
3	Keeping the project in line with customer strategies.	C	Senior Supplier
4	Recording and tracking Project Issues.	D	Project Assurance
5	Advising on design and development aspects.	E	Project Manager
6	Ensuring quality assurance standards are being adhered to.	F	Team Manager
7	Responsible for Change Control and Configuration Management.	G	Project Support
8	Prioritising user requirements.		

Syllabus Area	Question Number	Part	Marks
Quality in a project environment	9	B	24

A Label will be put on the Envelope. The Label must avoid the idea that the Envelope contains junk mail. It should be self-adhesive, half the size of the Selected Envelope (+/-5%), give the idea that the Envelope contains a useful present, and use an attractive, large font for the customer's name and address and the sender. The standard Company Logo needs to be integrated into the Label.

Column 1 is a list of information that may be relevant for the Product Description of the Label. Determine whether each item of information is relevant and select the appropriate Product Description heading from Column 2 where it should be recorded. A selection from Column 2 may be used more than once or not at all.

	Column 1		Column 2
1	Half the size of the Selected Envelope	A	Purpose
2	Selected Envelope	B	Composition
3	Quality Review	C	Derivation
4	Sender's name	D	Format and presentation
5	Glossy Paper	E	Quality criteria
6	Label Competition	F	Quality method
7	+/-5% in size	G	Quality tolerance

8	Company Logo	H	Quality check skills and/or people required
9	Self-adhesive	I	Not relevant
10	Give the idea that the Envelope contains a useful present		
11	Ready by 30 November		
12	Selection by Marketing Director		

Syllabus Area	Question Number	Part	Marks
Quality in a project environment	9	C	12

Lines 1 to 4 in the table below consist of an assertion statement and a reason statement. For each line identify the appropriate selection from options A to E that applies. A selection may be used more than once or not at all.

Selection	Assertion	Reason	
A	True	True	Reason is a correct explanation of the assertion
B	True	True	Reason is correct but not an explanation for the assertion
C	True	False	
D	False	True	
E	False	False	

	Assertion		Reason
1	Project Assurance should check that the Quality Log is being updated and that quality standards are applied correctly.	BECAUSE	Quality standards from both the customer and the supplier should be considered.
2	Quality assurance should help outline the Business Case.	BECAUSE	The quality assurance function should ensure that the project fits with overall company strategy.
3	Project Assurance should review any external Team Manager plans.	BECAUSE	Project Assurance should verify that planned quality-checking of products is satisfactory.
4	A quality assurance function should be separate from and independent of the organisation's project and operational activities.	BECAUSE	Quality assurance should monitor use of the quality system across projects within the corporate body.

Sample PRINCE2 Practitioner Objective Test Marking Scheme

DX01

Plans	Question	Part	A	B	C	D	E	F	G	H	I
	1	A	A	B	C	D	E	F	G	H	I
		1	-0.5	0.5	0.5	-0.5					
		2	0.5	-0.5	-0.5	-0.5					
		3	0.5	-0.5	-0.5	-0.5					
		4	-0.5	-0.5	0.5	-0.5					
	Question	Part									
	1	B	A	B	C	D	E	F	G	H	I
		1		1			2				
		2					1	2			
		3				1			1	2	
		4		2							1
		5				1			2	2	
		6				2					
		7			2						
		8	1								2
		9			2					1	
		10							2	1	
	Question	Part									
	1	C	A	B	C	D	E	F	G	H	I
		1					3				
		2					3				
		3				3					
		4		3							
		5	3								
		6					3				

Risk	Question	Part									
	2	A	A	B	C	D	E	F	G	H	I
		1			2	2					
		2	2								
		3	1	2							
		4					2				
		5		2			1				
		6				2					
		7		2							
		8		2	1						
	Question	Part									
	2	B	A	B	C	D	E	F	G	H	I
		1	3								
		2		3							
		3				3					
		4			3						
		5			3						
		6					3				
		7	3								
		8					3				

Controls	Question	Part									
	3	A	A	B	C	D	E	F	G	H	I
		1	-1	-1	1						
		2	-1	-1	1						
		3	1	1	1						
		4	-1	-1	1						
	Question	Part									
	3	B	A	B	C	D	E	F	G	H	I
		1			2						
		2					2				
		3					2				
		4					2				
		5		2							
		6				2					
		7	2								
		8				2					
	Question	Part									
	3	C	A	B	C	D	E	F	G	H	I
		1					3				
		2		3							
		3	3								

		4			3						
		5				3					
		6			3						

PBP	Question	Part									
	4	A	A	B	C	D	E	F	G	H	I
		1	2								
		2		2	1						
		3	2								
		4				2					
		5			2						
	Question	Part									
	4	B	A	B	C	D	E	F	G	H	I
		1									3
		2									3
		3						3			
		4									3
		5	3								
		6									3
		7			3						
		8		3	1						
		9				3					
		10									3

Config Mgmt	Question	Part									
	5	A	A	B	C	D	E	F	G	H	I
		1			2						
	Question	Part									
	5	B	A	B	C	D	E	F	G	H	I
		1						2			
		2								2	
		3					2				
		4			2	2					
		5					2				
		6							2		
		7		2					2		
	Question	Part									
	5	C	A	B	C	D	E	F	G	H	I
		1			3						
		2						3			
		3	3								

		4							3		
		5	3								
		6					3				
		7								3	
		8								3	

Change Control	Question	Part									
	6	A	A	B	C	D	E	F	G	H	I
		1	5								
	Question	Part									
	6	B	A	B	C	D	E	F	G	H	I
		1	0.5	-0.5							
		2	-0.5	0.5							
		3	-0.5	0.5							
		4	0.5	-0.5							
		5	0.5	-0.5							
		6	-0.5	0.5							
		7	-0.5	0.5							
		8	0.5	-0.5							
		9	0.5	-0.5							
		10	0.5	-0.5							
	Question	Part									
	6	C	A	B	C	D	E	F	G	H	I
		1	2								
		2			2	1					
		3	2								
		4		2							
		5		2							
		6				2					
	Question	Part									
	6	D	A	B	C	D	E	F	G	H	I
		1		3							
		2				3					
		3				3					
		4					3				
		5	3								
		6	3								

Processes	Question	Part									
	7	A	A	B	C	D	E	F	G	H	I
		1	0.5	-0.5							
		2	-0.5	0.5							
		3	0.5	-0.5							
		4	0.5	-0.5							
		5	-0.5	0.5							
		6	0.5	-0.5							
	Question	Part									
	7	B	A	B	C	D	E	F	G	H	I
		1				2					
		2	2	1							
		3								2	
		4				2					
		5				2					
		6		1			2				
		7								2	
		8		2							
		9		1		2					
		10				2					
		11					2				
	Question	Part									
	7	C	A	B	C	D	E	F	G	H	I
		1			3						
		2					3				
		3				3					
		4	3								
		5					3				

Business Case	Question	Part									
	8	A	A	B	C	D	E	F	G	H	I
		1	1	-1	-1	-1	-1	-1			
		2	-1	1	-1	-1	-1	-1			
		3	-1	-1	-1	1	-1	-1			
		4	-1	1	-1	-1	1	-1			
		5	1	-1	-1	-1	-1	-1			
		6	-1	1	-1	-1	-1	-1			
	Question	Part									
	8	B	A	B	C	D	E	F	G	H	I
		1	-0.5	0.5							
		2	0.5	-0.5							
		3	-0.5	0.5							
		4	-0.5	0.5							
		5	-0.5	0.5							
		6	0.5	-0.5							
		7	-0.5	0.5							
		8	-0.5	0.5							
	Question	Part									
	8	C	A	B	C	D	E	F	G	H	I
		1	2								
		2						2			
		3				2					
		4			2						
		5				2					
		6							2		
		7		2							
		8			2						
		9							2		
	Question	Part									
	8	D	A	B	C	D	E	F	G	H	I
		1	1	3							
		2			3						
		3			3						
		4	3								

Quality	Question	Part									
	9	A	A	B	C	D	E	F	G	H	I
		1	-0.5	-0.5	-0.5	0.5	-0.5	-0.5	-0.5		
		2	-0.5	-0.5	0.5	0.5	-0.5	-0.5	-0.5		
		3	0.5	-0.5	-0.5	-0.5	-0.5	-0.5	-0.5		
		4	-0.5	-0.5	-0.5	-0.5	-0.5	-0.5	0.5		
		5	-0.5	-0.5	0.5	-0.5	-0.5	-0.5	-0.5		
		6	-0.5	-0.5	-0.5	0.5	-0.5	-0.5	-0.5		
		7	-0.5	-0.5	-0.5	-0.5	0.5	-0.5	-0.5		
		8	-0.5	0.5	-0.5	-0.5	-0.5	-0.5	-0.5		
	Question	Part									
	9	B	A	B	C	D	E	F	G	H	I
		1				2	2				
		2			2						
		3						2			
		4		2							
		5									2
		6			2						
		7							2		
		8		2	1		1				
		9				2	2				
		10	2				2				
		11									2
		12								2	
	Question	Part									
	9	C	A	B	C	D	E	F	G	H	I
		1		3							
		2					3				
		3	3								
		4	3								

And finally . . .

If you've managed to get this far you are as ready for the PRINCE2 examinations as you are ever likely to be. It remains only to wish you the little bit of luck that we all need to make a success of any venture in life. If you are still not confident of your knowledge of PRINCE2, or your ability to convince an examiner that you are able to apply it to a given situation, you should consider attending an APM Group accredited training event and, perhaps, try to gain more experience in using the method.

Good luck with your preparation.

September 2007

Index